Confronting Gangs

Crime and Community

G. David Curry

Scott H. Decker

University of Missouri—St. Louis

Foreword by C. Ronald Huff

Roxbury Publishing Company
Los Angeles, California

7-31-98

Curry, G. David
Confronting gangs: crime and community/G. David Curry, Scott
  H. Decker
  p. cm.
  Includes bibliographical references and index.
  ISBN 0-935732-92-6
  1. Gangs—United States. 2. Juvenile delinquency—United States.
  I. Decker, Scott H. II. Title
  HV6439.U5C85 1998
  364.1'06'60973—dc21   97-28935
                                                         CIP

Confronting Gangs: Crime and Community

Publisher and Editor: Claude Teweles
Copy Editor: Robert Watrous
Production Editors: Kate Sterner, C. Max-Ryan
Production Coordinator: Renee Burkhammer
Cover Design: Marnie Deacon Kenney
Cover Photos: Courtesy of Scott H. Decker and Dietrich L. Smith
Typography: Synergistic Data Systems

Printed on acid-free paper in the United States of America. This paper
meets the standards for recycling of the Environmental Protection
Agency.

ISBN: 0-935732-92-6

Roxbury Publishing Company
P.O. Box 491044
Los Angeles, California 90049-9044
Tel: (213) 653-1068 • Fax: (213) 653-4140
Email: roxbury@crl.com

Contents

Acknowledgements

I f it takes a village to raise a child, it takes a huge village to write a book. We are grateful for the cooperation and insight of a number of our colleagues throughout the process of writing this book. Several veteran gang researchers have also provided encouragement and guidance through the years, and their input helped shape our perspective on gangs. Jim Short, Malcolm Klein, Ron Huff, Mark Fleisher, Cheryl Maxson, and Irv Spergel are wellsprings of information and inspiration that influence the way we think and write about gang problems.

Additionally, ten talented individuals read the book in manuscript form and offered comments that helped improve the finished product. They are: Dean J. Champion (Minot State University), John M. Hagedorn (University of Illinois-Chicago), Randy Blazak (Portland State), Finn-Aage Esbensen (University of Nebraska-Omaha), Marjorie S. Zatz (Arizona State University), Irving A. Spergel (University of Chicago), Thomas J. Bernard (Pennsylvania State University), Scott Menard (University of Colorado-Boulder), Pamela Irving Jackson (Rhode Island College), and Meda Chesney-Lind (University of Hawaii-Manoa). We hope we have met the high standards set in their comments.

Several colleagues participated in the actual process of collecting, editing, and typing materials for the book. Patricia Tierney helped navigate a world of symbols in helping with copyediting the manuscript. Dietrich Smith was an able field assistant, providing research insights and photo opportunities. Cathy McNeal offered a variety of support efforts throughout the project. Our faculty colleague Richard Wright, ever the wordsmith, came up with the title for the book. And Jody Miller, our colleague, read and offered insightful comments on Chapter 5.

This book benefited significantly from the efforts of all these individuals.

We are also grateful to our families for putting up with the distractions of having a book completed in their midst. We are grateful to Janet and Zoe Curry; and JoAnn, Sara, Laura, and Elizabeth Decker for their understanding and patience. In a way, this book was written for them.

Foreword

by C. Ronald Huff

The book that you are about to read, written by two of the nation's most widely respected gang researchers, scholars, and educators, will introduce you to a very important and fascinating topic in modern society. You may or may not live in an area where gangs are visible, but whether you see them on a daily basis or not, gangs have a significant—and growing—impact on our communities. And it is communities that provide the context within which gangs are discussed in this book.

This community perspective is an important intellectual tradition in sociology and criminology—the "Chicago School" (at the University of Chicago)—which emphasized the importance of understanding the communities in which crime, juvenile delinquency, and gangs exist. The earliest study of American gangs, by Thrasher, was a product of the Chicago School, and this book is squarely in that important tradition.

Many of the key factors that explain the formation of gangs, why young people join gangs, and why gangs either survive or disband relate to the dynamics of the communities in which gangs and gang members exist. The authors' experience in interviewing gang members and in studying both gangs and community responses to gangs makes them highly qualified to write this book, and they skillfully utilize their field experience in their writing.

All too often, gangs are viewed in the abstract, without considering the interactions between gangs and communities and without taking a close look inside the gangs. This book does not make that mistake. Instead, "thick" context is provided to enhance and demystify the reader's knowledge of gangs. You will learn about gangs from the perspective of the gang members (often in their own words), the community, and the law enforcement officers who try to respond to gangs and the problems they pose for our communities.

In *Confronting Gangs*, Curry and Decker begin by defining the terms "gang" and "gang member." They help the reader understand the process of joining gangs and the full range of experience involved in belonging to gangs. They explain how some young people manage to leave gangs, address the complex issue of drug trafficking by gang members, and examine the involvement of females in gangs. The authors go on to explain the broader socioeconomic linkages and assess both public policy and programmatic initiatives that have been, or should be, undertaken to address gangs and gang-related crime. The book also gives some consideration to how adequately various theories of gangs hold up and how those theories might be improved in the light of recent research.

Many people tend to regard gangs as "the problem." In fact, gangs are actually a *symptom* of more causally important underlying problems in society. Research demonstrates that gang members are far more likely than nongang youth to become involved in serious and violent crime and to become chronic offenders. Risk factors that are associated with chronic gang crime underscore the importance of insuring that young people can grow up in healthy communities.

Throughout this valuable and easy-to-read book, Curry and Decker draw upon both classic and recent research and help the reader distinguish fact from fiction by pointing out some of the myths about gangs and gang members that are perpetuated by the media. To be successful, democratic societies must depend upon informed citizens to make intelligent personal and public policy choices about a wide range of social problems, including gangs. This book will help its readers do just that.

Introduction

Confronting Gangs introduces students to the topic of gangs. The book is designed for courses on gangs, delinquency, criminology, violence, social problems, juvenile justice, and criminal justice. Emphasizing community and neighborhood, Confronting Gangs weaves contemporary research and policy findings around classic and emerging theories of gangs. It provides students with links between the gang literature and traditional criminological, criminal justice, and sociological approaches to gangs. Gang members' perspectives on many issues are included through the use of quotes from the gang members themselves.

Our intent in writing this book was to provide a foundation from which students can learn more about gangs, gang members, and their many activities. This foundation is important not only for what it may reveal about social organization and processes; gangs are a significant public policy issue, and informed citizens have a better chance of playing constructive roles in the response to gangs.

We wrote this book from a particular perspective, in that we view the context of gang life as crucial for understanding the complexities of gang activities and organization. The most important aspect of the gang-life context is, in our view, the neighborhood or community in which gang members live and operate. Community context has long been a topic of concern among criminologists and sociologists as they attempt to understand both the forces that create social problems and the best way to develop effective interventions to address those problems. Throughout this book, we emphasize the features of the particular community in question that create a climate in which gangs are more likely to form, have an impact on the lives of gang members, and shape the nature of life in the gang.

This emphasis on community is associated with the Chicago School of sociology, an intellectual and research tradition that highlighted the role of social and demographic characteristics of neighborhoods in the creation of crime and delinquency. We believe that the solutions for solving the problem of gangs are most likely to come from the same communities that create them. Thus, our review of gang programs highlights the role of community agencies and characteristics in responding to gangs.

Confronting Gangs presents a large volume of research about gangs and gang members. The research is presented critically, that is, with an eye toward areas where consensus exists regarding findings. We use the results of research to better describe the gang problem and appropriate responses to that problem.

* * *

Confronting Gangs begins by describing the complex task of defining gangs and identifying who is a gang member. Most people take these definitions for granted, but the issues involved are complex. Without clear definitions, it is not possible to develop a broader understanding of the range of gang activities. These definitions then allow us to document the size and scope of the gang problem in the United States. A unique feature of Chapter 1 is its inclusion of the views of gang members from a number of cities.

Chapter 2 examines the link between gang membership and involvement in crime and delinquency. Gang membership clearly enhances criminal and delinquent involvement, and this chapter identifies the mechanisms through which this process works. We distinguish between involvement in minor forms of delinquency, such as vagrancy or shoplifting, and more serious crimes such as shootings and drug sales. The chapter draws heavily from community-based field studies of gangs.

Chapter 3 is devoted to describing the gang experience. We follow the process of joining gangs, gang initiation, involvement in violence, painting graffiti, and leaving gangs. As in earlier chapters, we present the perspectives of gang members on these issues through a series of quotes that reflect the meaning of these activities to individual gang members.

Much attention is focused on drug sales by gangs. We tackle this issue head on in Chapter 4. By comparing the different sources of information—gang members, nongang youth, police, and other public officials—we attempt to isolate the role that gangs and gang members play in drug sales. We then contrast two views about the extent to which gangs control drug sales, both generally and among their members.

Chapter 5 covers female gang involvement. This is a neglected but important topic, as the number of female gangs and gang members is growing, and female gang membership has broad implications. This chapter isolates some of the reasons why young women join gangs and their activities within gangs.

Gang members belong to a number of groups. The media tend to view them only as members of their particular gangs, but that view is short-sighted. Gang members also have families, attend school, hold jobs, and interact with individuals and groups in their neighborhoods. Chapter 6 provides some balance in the view of the lives of gang members by noting the social institutions they belong to and participate in, particularly their families.

Chapter 7 provides a comprehensive review of recent state and federal initiatives for dealing with gangs. We examine the characteristics of programs—how they were formulated and what they intend to accomplish—as well as their impact. The last decade has seen a flurry of programmatic activity directed toward reducing gang violence, drug sales, crime, and membership. This chapter provides a "report card" on how successful such interventions have been, as well as suggestions about how these programs might be improved.

The book concludes with Chaper 8, which offers the reader a series of issues to confront. Some of these issues concern theories explaining the development of gangs and gang activity, and they tie the preceding seven chapters together. In addition, we cover several policy initiatives which could be implemented in order to confront gangs successfully.

Both authors have extensive experience researching gangs and gang members. G. David Curry has worked with police and gang programs to conduct evaluations and surveys. Scott H. Decker has observed and interviewed hundreds of gang members. We combine these perspectives throughout the book to bring you the flavor of gang life, through the eyes of gang members themselves and agents of the criminal justice system who respond to gangs. We hope that at the book's conclusion readers will be better prepared to confront the reality of gangs.

Chapter One

Defining and Measuring the Prevalence of Gangs

Mike-Mike is a 20-year-old member of the Thundercats, a St. Louis gang that formed in a local public housing project. He is a black male who joined his gang at the age of 14 and has been heavily involved in drug sales and other crimes. He has been arrested ten times. Mike-Mike is a leader of the Thundercats, although he claims to be trying to get the younger guys in the gang to "slow down." In interviews, he admits that he is frightened by the reckless violence of younger gang members. Because of his two children, both under the age of 5, he is trying to withdraw from gang activity. But he finds that it is hard to do, as the younger gang members look to him for advice. He left St. Louis for Memphis as a way of trying to slow down, but ultimately returned to St. Louis.

At age 13, a youth named Tim was picked up by police a few miles from his near northwest Chicago home for tampering with an automobile. The next year, Tim became involved in a conflict with youths from a nearby middle school. Within two months, he was taken into custody twice for fighting on the grounds of the other school. Two weeks later he was apprehended for robbery, and the police recorded that the victim of the robbery was a known member of Chicago's Vice Lords gang. That summer Tim was ticketed, along with a number of youths, under Chicago's antiganging ordinance. All of the youths, including Tim, were identified in police records as Black Gangster Disciples. The following spring Tim, then aged 15, was charged as an offender in a gang-related aggravated assault. The following week, in a confrontation with his father in their home over Tim's gang involvement and trouble with the authori-

1

ties, Tim seriously injured his father and was again charged with aggra-
vated assault. During the following year Tim was charged twice with
criminal damage to property and once with unlawful use of a weapon.
Finally Tim moved into the adult criminal justice system.

W hy did these young people commit these acts? What role
did gang membership play in their lives? What can we do
about gangs?

This book is designed to help you understand these questions.
One of the ways we will approach gangs is to talk about the "pushes"
and "pulls" that produce gangs and gang members. By pushes, we
mean those forces that compel individuals to join gangs, and by
pulls, we mean those forces that individuals find attractive reasons
to join gangs. Pay careful attention to this distinction because it will
resurface throughout the book.

We begin this book by asking three simple questions:

What is a gang?
Who is a gang member?
What is a gang crime?

However, as we shall see in this chapter, and throughout the
book, these are not simple questions. Indeed, there is disagreement
about the answers to all three questions. And this disagreement is
not just an academic matter. For example, police in the two U.S. cities
most affected by gangs—Los Angeles and Chicago—differ greatly
in how they answer these questions. For these reasons, we begin
this book with a series of discussions about how gangs, gang members, and gang crimes are defined.

Defining a Gang

Most students are surprised to learn that there is no accepted or
straightforward definition of a gang. The situation is so muddled
that the U.S. Justice Department has stepped in to try and bring some
clarity to the definition of a gang. It has done so by holding a series
of meetings between police, researchers, policy makers, community
activists, and others involved in understanding and responding to
gangs. The results, so far, have not provided a definitive answer to
the question "What is a gang?"

There are a number of elements typically included in the definition of a gang. One thing at least everyone agrees on, any useful

definition of a gang must include a *group*. Some definitions of a gang specify the number of members. For example, the Los Angeles police and sheriff's departments both specify that a gang is a group of two or more individuals who meet a number of other criteria. However, as Malcolm Klein (1996) and Irving Spergel (1995) have both pointed out, seldom does a gang have as few as two members. Indeed, most research based on law enforcement estimates shows that gangs have a good deal more members than just two. And since most delinquent acts or crimes committed by juveniles are done in groups, distinguishing between groups and gangs is important.

A second element in defining gangs concerns the use of *symbols*. Most gangs have symbols of membership. These symbols can take a number of forms. Today clothes, hand signs, and certain ways of wearing clothes are among the most popular, and visible, gang symbols in this country. Most gang symbols only have meaning within the gang, and an effort is generally made to keep the meaning of symbols from becoming known by nongang strangers. However, there are times when symbols become so widely known, such as with the contemporary gangs the Bloods and Crips, that knowledge about gang signs and symbols is diffused throughout the population. Bloods are left-oriented and Crips are right-oriented. That is, Bloods tend to wear their hats to the left, hang a bandanna (also known as a rag) out of their left pocket, and refrain from using the letter "c," because it is the first letter of their rival's name. On the other hand, Crips wear their hats to the right, hang a rag out of their right pocket, and refrain from using the letter "b" because it is the first letter of the Bloods, their rivals.

Communication is another element of gangs. (We realize that symbols are a form of communication, but we choose to make this distinction, though some might view it as being an arbitrary one.) Most gangs have developed a series of verbal and nonverbal forms of communication. A variety of words have been developed by gangs, typically out of informal trial and error rather than as the result of a purposeful effort to develop such symbols. Nonverbal forms of communication include graffiti or hand signs. Hand signs can be very elaborate, often replacing verbal communication, particularly during confrontations between gangs.

Graffiti is used by gangs to communicate a variety of messages. According to Spergel (1995, p. 87), the role of graffiti varies across gangs, communities, and ethnic groups. Traditionally, gang graffiti has been viewed as a method of claiming territory. Ray Hutcheson (1993, p. 163), who has devoted more attention to the study of graffiti than most gang researchers, maintained that marking territory is not how all or most graffiti is used. Still, researchers have made some observations about how graffiti is used in claiming territory. Hutcheson (p. 162) pointed out that graffiti used to mark the external boundaries of a gang's territory is larger and easier to associate with a particular gang. Graffiti that is more central to a gang's territory is more elaborate and less apparent in its meaning to nongang members. Spergel (p. 87) observed that graffiti is more dense closer to the center of some gangs' turfs.

Hutcheson (1993, pp. 158–59) found a number of differences between the Latino gang graffiti that he studied both in Los Angeles and Texas and Latino gang graffiti in Chicago. While some Los Angeles gangs have been around for half a century, Chicago gangs have only existed for half that time. Hutcheson credited this difference in age of gangs for the more stylized and uniform lettering found in gang graffiti throughout the Southwest. In Chicago, he observed that gang graffiti involved more freeform lettering and it associated particular symbols with specific gangs. For example, the Latin Disciples represented themselves with a winged heart. The Insane Unknowns incorporated a ghost into their graffiti; the Latin Kings used a crown. Los Angeles gangs did not use such symbolic representations of their gangs in their graffiti.

Gang graffiti can also become a vehicle for gang confrontation (Decker, 1996, p. 130). Graffiti can be challenged by writing profanity over it or simply marking it out. The letter k for "kill" can be used to pepper one's own gang's graffiti with references to killing members of enemy gangs or can be applied to an opposing gang's graffiti to reverse its meaning (Sanders, 1994, p. 62.) "RIP" added to an opposing gang's graffiti provides an obvious message—Rest in peace (Decker, 1996, p. 132). In Chicago, where symbols were such an important part of gang graffiti, Hutcheson (1993, p. 162) observed that manipulation of these symbols in derogatory ways produced imaginative levels of artistic expression.

In their documentary film, Taggart Siegel and Dwight Conquergood (1990) captured the uses of graffiti by gang members very well, especially in memorializing dead gang comrades. As are many of the symbolic expressions of gang behavior, gang graffiti is an evolving mode of expression (Hutcheson, 1993; Sanders, 1994). Hutcheson (p. 138) suggests that the study of gang graffiti can tell us much about changes in gang structure, alliances, and conflicts.

In order to be defined as a gang, a group must have *permanence*, that is, it must be in existence for a period of time. Many confederations of young people form over a specific issue, only to be disbanded and never seen again. Most definitions of what a gang is require that the gang be in existence over a prolonged period of time, generally a year or more. This feature of gangs varies considerably, as some Chicago gangs have been in existence since the 1960s, and other gangs in Los Angeles have been around for nearly 60 years. Most gangs in America are considerably newer than that, and many of these new gangs have already come and gone.

A number of definitions of gangs include *turf*, or gang-identified territory, as a crucial element. There is some controversy about this feature of gangs, however. Many contemporary gangs do claim some territory as their own, either because it is where the gang began or where most of the members live. However, some gangs, particularly Asian gangs, do not claim turf, but otherwise meet all of the other criteria of a gang. For this reason, most definitions of a gang do not include turf, though most gangs claim turf.

The final element in defining a gang is involvement in *crime*. It is possible to imagine a large number of groups that meet the first five criteria of the definition of a gang. Indeed, you are probably a member of several groups that meet these criteria, and the authors of this book belong to several groups with their own symbols and specialized forms of communication that have been around for a long time and claim turf. However, these criteria alone do not make an academic department, the Biology Club, or an athletic team a gang. Rather, what distinguishes a gang from other groups is its involvement in crime. This is a very important distinction. We contend that a good definition of a gang must include involvement in crime as a feature of gang activities. Yet, as you will see later, the way we portray most gangs argues that they do not have well-developed ideologies, nor do they effectively organize and control their members. Gangs are heavily involved in crime and recognize that involvement as a key feature of gang membership.

We have said what a gang is, and it is probably just as important to say what a gang is not. We have restricted this book to the study of what Klein (1996) has identified as a street gang. We have done so in order to identify a manageable and coherent subject matter. We exclude hate groups, such as the Ku Klux Klan, organized crime groups like the Cosa Nostra, and antigovernment groups like the Michigan Militia. These exclusions have not been made because we believe these groups to be unimportant. Quite the contrary, we have studied and written about these groups in other contexts (Curry et al. 1997). However, our understanding and ability to respond to street gangs is enhanced when we define them in a fashion that produces a coherent, well-defined product.

Defining Gangs and Gang Members

Fortunately, defining a gang member is not so difficult as defining a gang. The most powerful measure of gang membership is self-nomination. By this we mean that simply asking individuals whether or not they belong to a gang —"claiming" in gang talk — is the best means of identifying who is a gang member. A large number of studies using diverse methodologies provide support for this contention. For example, the survey research conducted by Finn Esbensen and his colleagues (Esbensen and Huizinga, 1993), the interviews conducted by Scott Decker and his colleagues (Decker and Van Winkle, 1994, 1996; Decker, 1996) and the work using secondary data sources like police records conducted by Cheryl Maxson and Malcolm Klein (Maxson and Klein, 1994) all support this view. In the fields of sociology and criminology, such convergence across methods is rare indeed.

But there are other ways to determine if an individual is a member of a gang. A number of other symbols and behaviors can be used to distinguish gang members from nonmembers and "wanna-bes." Police departments across the country keep detailed records of the names of gang members, and these can be a valuable source of information about the identifies of some gang members. However, there are shortcomings to using police files for research because such information can be dated, based on misinformation, or fail to reflect changes in gang affiliation by individuals. And, as Ronald Huff (1996) has observed, the overidentification of gang members can have significant negative consequences. When an individual has made the decision and taken the steps to leave a gang, but is still in a police gang database and treated by the police as a gang member, rival members may continue to perceive that individual as an active member and attack him as if he were still a gang member.

But police and other official records are not the only way to identify gang members. Asking gang members and neighborhood residents, especially youths or teachers, to identify gang-involved people can provide another way to determine who is in a gang. Gang members often bear the symbols of their gang affiliation. Certainly the presence of gang tattoos is an indicator of gang involvement. The decision to get a gang tattoo represents an important step for gang involvement and is often reserved only for the most involved members. In many gangs a tattoo conveys a certain status or credibility to members, and members are only eligible for such marking after extensive involvement in gang activities. A tattoo is perhaps the most severe outward indication of membership, but there are others. The company an individual keeps can also be a key to establishing whether or not he or she is involved in the gang.

A good deal of attention in our society is paid to gang clothes. Gang members display a distinctive method of dress and demeanor that at one time distinguished them from their nongang peers. However, due to the influence of popular culture—especially the influencing of clothing styles through the movies, music videos, and magazines—gang styles now enjoy widespread popularity. Sagging pants, distinctive blue or red clothing, shirts buttoned only at the top, and the popularity of certain brand names no longer can be used reliably to distinguish gang members from their nongang style-conscious peers.

Now a word about "wanna-bes." We do not really like to use this term when referring to gang members or young people who may imitate gang behavior or styles but are not fully initiated members. In the late 1980s, a number of cities (such as Cleveland, Columbus, and St. Louis) denied that they had real gang problems and real gang members by dismissing the obvious signs of such activities as simply the product of wanna-bes. These efforts were counterproductive because they let gang members gain a foothold in their communities, and, as a consequence, it was more difficult to respond to the problems they created, and minimized the influence of gangs. Instead, we prefer to distinguish between core and fringe members.

Core members represent self-acknowledged gang members who have been members for more than a year and are actively involved in the commission of crimes with other gang members. In addition, such individuals tend to be older, certainly around age 16. Fringe gang members, on the other hand, have less involvement in the activities of the gang and are less often involved in key gang activities such as drive-by shootings, initiations, and, when they occur, meetings. This should not diminish the importance of such fringe members, for they can create havoc and violence just as easily as a core gang member. As a young gang member being held for a crime in the St. Louis juvenile detention center told us:

> There ain't no such thing as a wanna-be. He can shoot, he can kill you just like a real gang member.

Our approach to defining gangs and gang members draws heavily from our experiences interviewing and interacting with gang members. Over the years we have interviewed gang members in St. Louis; San Diego; Chicago; Inglewood, California; Pueblo, Colorado; Seattle; Boston; and Washington, D.C. We have learned a good deal about how gang membership is defined by those individuals whose lives are most affected by gang membership. Here we present the views of some of those individuals to illustrate the two dimensions most gang members use to describe a gang: (1) criminal involvement and (2) aspects of friendship that border on descriptions of the gang as a family.

In St. Louis most gang members defined their gang in terms of criminal involvement. There is a considerable amount of bravado in their descriptions of a gang.

> If you want to be a real gang member you got to bust out windows, steal, sell dope, hang out. The next one you got to do if you in the gang, you got to sell coke or rock, anything. They think it [gang membership] is fun, they can rule everything, take over schools, take over neighborhoods and they think they own all that.

> Having a reputation and having people terminated, shot up, show off, pretend like you bad, want everybody to stay away from you cause you don't want to express your feelings.

> Just be fighting [to be a gang member]. You feel like you got it, feel tougher. That's all I can say. Beat everybody up, be fighting

and if somebody try to beat you up then the whole gang will jump in.

Somebody who is fighting over colors. Somebody approach me and say, "What's up Blood?" and I'm going to say "Killer." They down on my set, they know I'm a Crip. If they come here and say "What's up Blood?" I'm going to say "Killer." That mean I'm a killer. Then we will probably fight or shoot or whatever. Whatever happen it happen.

It's mainly protection. If I'm gonna sell some dope then I got somebody to protect me. Like if a Blood or Crip try to fight me then I have some protection so we won't get no interference. If the police come I can get away quicker while they be fighting.

Business, acting crazy. My friends, well they not really friends, but when it's time to go bangin' they'll help you out. When you ain't got no place to go they'll take you in. I ain't legit for real. It's easy money.

You can get to fight whoever you want and shoot whoever you want. To me it's kind of fun, then again it's kind of not because you have to go to jail for that shit. I'm tired of that. But other than that, being down for who you want to be with, it's kind of fun.

Other St. Louis members talked about the importance of group attributes. Typically they described the gang as a family, or a loosely based organization of friends who knew they could count on each other.

It feels kind of good [to be a gang member] 'cause you know on one hand you got two families. You got your family and then they all look at you like family. For instance, I get in some trouble and I can make more phone calls and I can be out of here but I don't want that. I can do this now but then on the other hand if I get into some trouble on the streets, it might cause a friend getting killed, it might cause me getting killed but we all stick together like family.

It's more like a family away from home. You with your friends, you all stick together. They ain't going to let nothing happen to you, you ain't going to let nothing happen to them.

To my knowledge it's a group of fellas. Not just fellas but ones that can depend on each other that's all down for the same thing.

Second family. A crew, family, cause it's together. A gang of people always together.

The Chicago gangs we interviewed reported a very different picture about gang membership. Our interviews in Chicago took place with two different groups, the Gangster Disciples and the Latin Kings, gangs that are more organized and have older membership. The Gangster Disciples is a black gang that emerged in the 1960s, and is considered to be among the most organized and largest in the country. GD's (as they refer to themselves) typically described the gang as an organization. Indeed, many gang members bristled at the characterization of their group as a gang, believing that such a term unfairly characterized them in negative terms.

> They are a consolidated group of people that are working toward one goal, to better the political social and economical development. I don't look at is as no gang because a gang, I always look at it as a wild radical group of people but we never acted like that.
>
> Some individuals look at it as being called Gangster Disciples but I don't look at it like that. I look at it as being a growth and development organization.
>
> Just like a business. The way they operate businesses is the same way we do it in ours. We have different people doing different things. It's not all running around shooting guns and sticking people up and selling drugs and stuff.
>
> Everybody be protesting on the news about it's a bunch of gang bangers and all that and like I just told you a little while ago, the organization, yeah sure enough, everybody out there call themself in a gang but it's like we come together. Everybody that's in it is not in it just to go out here and make trouble. They set examples for kids and try to help people out. Even the big time drug dealers that I'm not gonna get into here that people don't know, trying to help out.

But many members of the Gangster Disciples did use criminal involvement to define their gang.

> Well, in my words, a gang ain't nothing but people come together to do crime and make money and be a family to each other. I guess society put that label, it's a gang. I can speak for the Gangster Disciples and say that now the concept is to be productive, become educated, educate your community, doing things which is right. That's the new concept. I agree with they new direction.

I would personally consider it [a gang] a mob of individuals led by a chief or a king that's predominately a criminal activity though there may be ones that are trying to do something productive and do something for the community and things, but those are few and far in between. Especially they be involved in illegal activity also.

They getting pimped around for they little old money, little dudes and all that and they ain't really reaping nothing up out of it. It was like, back when I got hooked up, it was maybe because my older brother and them was into it and I was like OK, cool, I'm gonna get into this here. Now you got grammar school kids taking guns and crap to school talking about they in this gang. It's stupid, it don't make no sense, it's crazy.

Latin Kings reported many similar definitions of their gang. But they differed from the Gangster Disciples in two important respects. First, Kings emphasized the cultural aspects of their gang, stressing the familial nature of the gang. Perhaps as a consequence, Latin Kings were far less politicized than their African American counterparts in Chicago.

It's a second family. They are like your brothers. They will help you out when you need help. Whenever you mess up they will take care of you too. To me it's like a family, some people want to get out of it, they don't want to be a part of it no more.

Family, they are always there.

It's a group of brothers that agree to go by a set of rules or guidelines. We don't just do gang type tactics, just go beat people up. We have rules.

Other Latin Kings included involvement in crime as a major factor in their definition of a gang.

We have colors, we have our hand signs, our handshakes, and we represent against our enemies.

I think a gang is a way to escape reality, to tell you the truth. It's like an easier way to cope with life. When you are gang banging you are serious but there is a lot of people that are not serious when they join because they think it is cool and maybe sometimes most of the time when kids are young they join for that reason, to be cool and they end up doing time for the Latin Kings or going to jail or getting shot and having to rely on them.

San Diego gangs were less organized than those we interviewed in Chicago or St. Louis. However, Latino/a gangs did maintain a stronger orientation to family and group than did their African American counterparts. We interviewed members of the Syndo Mob, an African American gang in San Diego. This group emphasized criminal involvement in their definition of gangs.

> To me, a gang is you don't give a fuck and you are just right there with your homeboys, you know, partying. All you do is party and sell drugs. If you hit it off wrong with somebody else from another neighborhood you just do what you got to do.
>
> A gang is something where people get together and get in trouble, fights or whatever. One neighborhood has problems with somebody else's neighborhood.
>
> A gang in my opinion is like, I don't really call it a gang. I call it homies, I don't really call it a gang because I wear a green rag or something like that because that's the way I've been living. Yeah, of course they rob and kill and steal and do all that kind of stuff too, but that's only not necessarily everybody from Lincoln go out and kill.

A few members of this gang did identify affiliational characteristics of gangs.

> That was the only thing I had to look forward to. If I needed a place to stay I would go to them. When I was getting in trouble, to me, it felt like they were always there for me when I was little. Things got different when I got older. That's how I felt when I was younger. It's a family, it's like a group of friends that you grew up with.
>
> A gang to me is just a bunch of friends, just a bunch of people that grew up together as kids.
>
> What is a gang? A gang, to me, is a group of people that represent something like the area, the neighborhood, the community where they live and that, to me, would be a gang of people, from a certain neighborhood.

Calle Triente, also known as the Red Steps, was a Chicano gang in San Diego. Membership and gang definition issues among these individuals reflected a cultural orientation to ethnicity and family. In this manner, they were like their Latino/a counterparts in Chicago, the Latin Kings.

A gang is where you hang out. Your friends, you find a lot of love that you don't get at home, a lot of respect, they are always there for you.

Just my homeboys, the people that I hang around with, grew up with, family just like almost, friends. Most of them is family.

Yeah because when I was growing up I grew up on the streets and in juvenile hall. I never had nobody to tell me anything like stay home, go to school. They were there for me. I kind of fit in with them. If anything happens to them I feel hurt. We call ourselves like a real big family. Especially inside the system.

It's just like a neighborhood, some place you belong to. To some people a gang means everything. The gang bangers and the regular gang members they stay down for the neighborhood or someone who is just down for the neighborhood when they want to be.

Fewer members of this gang identified criminal involvement as the benchmark of gang membership, and many of them included elements of the family in those descriptions.

They are like a family. [But] my experience with a gang is trouble. They are not a company that works or anything. They sell drugs. Everybody know they are that way. That's why society is scared of them.

The first thing that comes to my mind is fighting with sticks and chains and stuff like that. I always wanted to be somebody that everybody thought was tough.

In sum, most gang members define their gang along one of two basic definitional lines: (1) involvement in crime or (2) the affiliational and cultural aspects of gang membership that make it like a family in the eyes of many members.

The History of Gangs

Are gangs new? Have gangs emerged in the 1980s and 1990s as a new form of youth culture and crime group not seen before? Are gangs a uniquely American phenomenon? The answers to these questions may surprise you. Gangs are *not* new, and in fact are found increasingly all over the world. The best evidence indicates that youth gangs, at least as we would define them now, have existed in the United States since at least the 1870s, and have seen four distinct periods of growth and peaks since that time. Klein (1995) has observed that cycles of gang activity vary by history as well as type of gang, geographic location, and ethnicity. As cities experienced immigration and industrial development in the latter part of the 19th century, most saw an increase in the origins of organized adolescent groups heavily involved in crime that can be identified as gangs. New York, Philadelphia, Boston, Chicago, St. Louis, and Pittsburgh—all experienced the emergence of gangs in the late 1800s. These gangs, described primarily by journalists, religious leaders, and social welfare groups, were disorganized aggregations of recent immigrants. In most cases, Italians and Irish immigrants were overrepresented in the ranks of gang members. These gangs roamed the streets of their neighborhoods, largely as disorganized groups, engaging primarily in petty forms of property crime and directing violence against one another and members of rival gangs. It is significant for our current understanding of gangs to note that these gangs were comprised of individuals from the bottom of the economic and cultural scale in their respective cities, not unlike the nature of gang membership today.

Interestingly, the gangs of the late 19th century died out without large-scale interventions by criminal justice or social service agencies. However, one generation down the road, approximately during the 1920s, the next generation of gangs emerged in American cities. It is important to distinguish between the youth gangs of the 1920s and their more organized adult counterparts, organized crime, also known as the mob. The youth gangs of the 1920s had far more in common with their earlier predecessors than they did with such notable gangsters as Al Capone, Bugsy Siegel, and Bugsy Malone. Most of the youth gang members of the 1920s were in disorganized groups, comprised of recent immigrants, typically the children of first generation immigrants. These gangs had symbols of membership and were more actively involved in crime than were their counterparts of a generation earlier. Indeed, the literature about these gangs is replete with references to their turf protection, violence (albeit with fist and knives, not sophisticated firearms as is the case today) and general property crime. These gangs also faded from the scene, apparently without substantial involvement on the part of the criminal justice system or social service agencies.

The next incarnation of gangs occurred during the 1960s. In many ways, these gangs represented a distinct break with the gangs of the 1890s and the 1920s. For the first time, significant numbers of racial minorities were involved in gang activities. However, the economic and demographic parallels between gang involvement in the 1960s and earlier gangs is suggestive of the importance of the underlying causes of gang membership. African Americans and Latinos were heavily represented in the gangs of the 1960s, and like their earlier counterparts, these individuals generally were located at the bottom of the social and economic ladders of American society.

But there were important differences between many of the gangs in the 1960s and their predecessors of the 1920s and the 1890s. First, these new gangs were more extensively involved in criminal activity, especially violence. The availability of guns and automobiles gave these gangs more firepower and the mobility to interact with and fight gangs in neighborhoods across a city. The more extensive involvement in crime, in turn, led to increased convictions and prison time. As a consequence, the prison became an important site for the growth and perpetuation of gangs. In Illinois and California in particular, the prison became an important site for the recruitment of gang members. As those prison gang members were released and returned to their communities, they brought gang ideology and practices with them. For cities like Los Angeles and Chicago, this helped produce intergenerational gangs, gangs that spanned more than one generation. Thus many neighborhoods found themselves with gang members ("OGs," original gangsters) in their 30s and 40s who were the parents of younger gang members. This makes responding to gangs more difficult, as older residents encourage and facilitate gang membership and development in their neighborhoods, and gangs come to be viewed as normal features of neighborhoods.

We mentioned earlier in this chapter that gangs are not confined to American society. Indeed, during World War II, "swing kids," young Germans who listened to American swing music, were identified as gangs owing to their deviant behavior, which often flaunted the authority of their parents and the government. Gangs have been reported in many of the nations that emerged from the breakup of the former Soviet Union and Soviet bloc nations. Sarajevo, in addition to being plagued by civil war and "ethnic cleansing," also has emerging youth gangs. Russia has a growing number of youth gangs as well as more organized adult crime groups that more closely resemble organized crime. Klein (1996) has documented the growing number of nations plagued by emerging youth gangs. The role of popular culture, particularly in the export of American cultural images through movies, music, and other media, has had an important impact on this development.

Counting Gangs, Gang Members, and Gang Crimes

Counting the number of gangs, gang members, and gang crimes is difficult. To be honest, we have estimates of the number of each of these things, not the "true" numbers. But over time, the methods used to estimate the count of each category have improved, and most observers feel that the data generally are reliable in providing estimates of how many gang members, gangs, and gang crimes there are in America.

When one of the authors (Curry) first began studying gangs, he shared a misconception held by many of his fellow citizens about records on youth gangs. He assumed there was a large database maintained by the FBI or some other federal authority in which all of the available information on gang members and gang-related crime resided. Data on gangs were imagined to be updated routinely in much the way that the Uniform Crime Report is updated annually. This, of course, has never been the case. Only recently has the federal government become interested in developing such databases on gangs, gang members, or gang-related crimes. Most of what we know about the national statistics on the gang problem is the product of a series of surveys conducted by different researchers over the last 25 years. Here we briefly review their methods and findings.

Walter Miller, The National Youth Gang Survey (1974–75)

The first study of the nation's gang problem was published in 1975. Walter Miller (1975) was a Harvard anthropologist who had conducted research on gangs and delinquency in Boston and other cities. Miller used population size, the nature of available local information on gangs, and an effort to achieve "some order of regional representation" to select 12 large U.S. cities to examine the scope of the national gang problem.

Each interview that Miller (p. 7) conducted began with the question "In your judgement, is there a 'gang problem' in this city?" From the answers he received, Miller (p. 9) constructed his definition of a gang:

> A gang is a group of recurrently associating individuals with identifiable leadership and internal organization, identifying with or claiming control over territory in the community, and engaging either individually or collectively in violent or other forms of illegal behavior.

Miller classified six of his 12 1975 cities as "gang problem" cities, as shown in Figure 1-1. At the time of this first national-level study, Miller (1975, p. 18) estimated that there were between 760 and 2,700 gangs and 28,500 to 81,500 gang members in those six cities. From his study of the six cities, Miller (pp. 21–22) concluded that gang members ranged in age from 12 to 21 and that "arrests of female gang members have generally been far fewer than those of males, and their criminality tends to be substantially less serious" (p. 23). Although most gang activity continued to be reported in inner-city areas, Miller (pp. 24–25) found evidence that gang activity had in some locales moved to the outer edges and suburbs of major cities.

Figure 1-1
Gang and Nongang Localities in Miller's 1975 National Survey

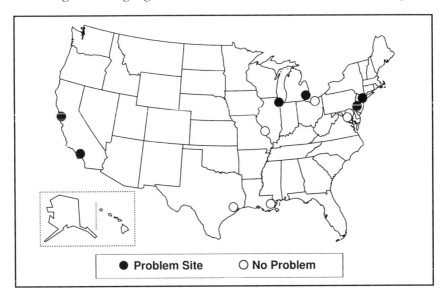

Walter Miller, The National Youth Gang Survey (1974–82)

Miller's (1982) second study of the gang problem extended the first to include interviews with 173 agencies in 26 intensive study sites. This time Miller selected a number of the localities based on newspaper and other media reports of gang activity in them. He identified only nine cities with gang problems. The geographic distribution of these cities is shown in Figure 1-2. From his analysis of the information that he collected from the wider range of cities, Miller concluded that 18 (50 percent) of the 36 urban areas with populations over 1 million had a gang problem at some point in the 1970s. In 1982, Miller projected a national estimate of 97,940 gang members in gangs located in 286 cities. He found the largest concentration of gangs to be in California (more than 30 percent of all U.S. gangs). Miller also reported a significant relationship between the presence of reported gang problems and city size, except in California. He suggested that this greater prevalence of gangs in smaller California cities might presage a future spread of gang problems to smaller-sized cities for the nation as a whole.

Figure 1-2
Gang and Nongang Localities in Miller's 1982 National Survey

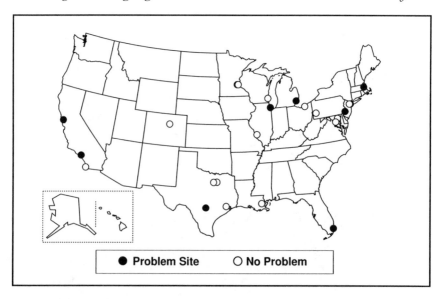

● **Problem Site**   ○ **No Problem**

Needle and Stapleton, Police Handling of Youth Gangs (1983)

Jerome A. Needle and William Vaughan Stapleton conducted a national study called *Police Handling of Youth Gangs*. They surveyed 60 police departments in cities across the country. The geographic distribution of these cities is shown in Figure 1-3. They used the following question to identify cities with a gang problem: *"Do you have youth gangs in your community or jurisdiction?"* Of the 60 police departments, 27 (45 percent) responded affirmatively about the presence of youth gangs in their jurisdictions. Needle and Stapleton argued that the dimensions of the national gang problem should be measured in terms of the numbers of gang-related crimes rather than numbers of gangs or members. They were frustrated, however, to discover that most police officials could not provide them with statistical information on crimes attributed to gang members.

Figure 1-3
Gang and Nongang Cities in Needle and Stapleton's 1983 National Survey

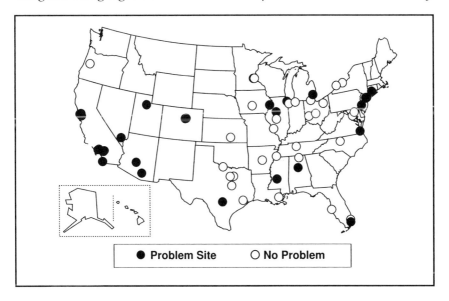

Spergel and Curry, The National Youth Gang Suppression and Intervention Program (1988)

The National Youth Gang Suppression and Intervention Program (to be described in greater detail in Chapter 7) conducted a national survey in 1988. Of the 98 cities or localities screened, 76 percent had organized gangs or gang activities. The geographic distribution of these cities is shown in Figure 1-4. Spergel and Curry (1993) broke the 45 cities with both gang problems and an organized response to the problem into two categories: 21 cities with chronic gang problems and 24 cities with emerging gang problems. Chronic gang problem cities "often had a long history of serious gang problems," and emerging gang problem cities were "often smaller cities that had recognized and begun to deal with an usually less serious but often acute gang problem since 1980." For 35 of the jurisdictions in their study where estimates were available, the researchers reported 1,439 gangs and 120,636 gang members.

Figure 1-4
Gang and Nongang Cities in Spergel and Curry's 1988 National Survey

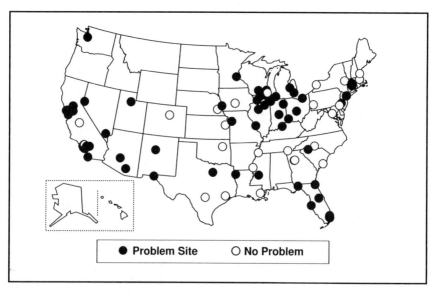

● **Problem Site**   ○ **No Problem**

Curry, Ball, and Fox, The National Assessment of Law Enforcement Anti-Gang Information Resources (1992)

In 1991, the task of arriving at national estimates of the magnitude of the gang problem was undertaken by Curry, Ball, and Fox (1994a). In addition to estimating the distribution and scope of the national-level gang crime problem, this study was designed to assess the quality of gang information resources available to local law enforcement. Each police department in the study was asked if their agency identified gangs as engaging in criminal activity within their jurisdiction. For the purposes of inclusion in the study, gangs were identified as meeting all of three criteria: (1) groups called "gangs" by law enforcement, (2) groups involving some level of participation by juveniles, and (3) groups engaging in criminal activity. If the answer was negative, the representative was asked if there were groups other than gangs that involved juveniles and engaged in criminal activity. In addition to this definitional screening criteria, available official definitions of gangs were obtained from each participating jurisdiction to be used in an analysis of gang definitions.

Of the 79 largest city police departments in the national assessment survey, 91 percent reported the presence of criminally involved groups that they labeled as gangs in their jurisdictions. Of the seven jurisdictions not reporting gang problems, 4 percent reported the presence of "gang-like," criminally involved, youth-based groups that were officially identified by some label other than gangs. Baltimore reported a "drug organization" problem; Raleigh, a "posse" problem; and Washington, D.C., a "crew" problem. Police departments in Memphis, Newark, Pittsburgh, and Richmond reported the presence of no officially acknowledged gangs, posses, crews, or other groups. (Pittsburgh officially recognized its gang problem in June 1992, a month after data collection for the project ended.) For the survey, 95 percent of large U.S. city police departments reported the officially recognized presence of gangs, crews, posses, or drug organizations engaged in criminal activity and involving youths within their jurisdictions. The estimate of the U.S. gang problem for 1991 was 4,881 gangs, 249,324 gang members, and 46,359 gang incidents. The geographic distribution of the cities in the study is shown in Figure 1-5.

The 1992 National Institute of Justice (NIJ) survey found that 70 of the 72 large U.S. cities reporting gang problems offered a depart-

Figure 1-5
Gang and Nongang Cities in Curry, Ball, and Fox's 1992 National Survey

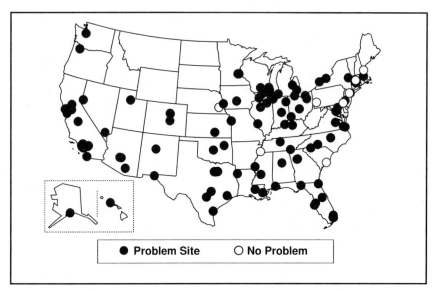

mental gang definition. Departments in three states—California, Florida, and Texas—reported following state legislative codes that define gangs. Over 30 other departments (some in the states with state codes) also supplied their own formal definitions of a gang.

The 1992 NIJ survey also attempted to gather available information on the age, ethnicity, and gender of gang members. Only a third of the departments surveyed could break their gang problems down in terms of crimes by adults and juveniles. There did seem to be a relationship between the age of a city's gang problem and the age of a city's gang member population. The breakdown of gang offenders by race and ethnicity was available for 37 metropolitan jurisdictions. Police records identified gang members as overwhelmingly African American and Latino/a at 48 percent and 43 percent, respectively. Asians Americans made up 5 percent and whites only 4 percent of gang members.

Curry, Ball, and Decker, The NIJ Extended National Assessment Survey (1994)

In 1994, another national survey (Curry et al., 1996) was conducted. This survey extended the 1992 survey by including all U.S.

cities ranging in population from 150,000 to 200,000 and a random sample of 284 municipalities ranging in population from 25,000 to 200,000. The results were tabulated by city size, a variable that was still found to have a relationship to the reported presence of gang crime problems. There were 76 U.S. cities with populations over 200,000 (as recorded in the 1990 census). Of these, 87 percent reported gang crime problems in 1994. (One of these, the District of Columbia, still officially labeled its problem a "crew" problem.) Combining city data with data from selected counties (reducing the number of gang members reported for Los Angeles County by one-fourth) resulted in a conservative estimate of 8,625 gangs, 378,807 gang members, and 437,066 gang crimes in the United States in 1993 based on local law enforcement records. The geographic distribution of the cities included in the study is shown in Figure 1-6.

Malcolm Klein, *The Study of Gang Problem Cities (Pre-1990–95)*

For a number of years, Malcolm Klein (1995) had been compiling a list of cities with gang crime problems. In 1991, he produced estimates of the scope of the national gang problem. Klein had identified

Figure 1-6
Gang and Nongang Cities in NIJ's 1994 National Survey

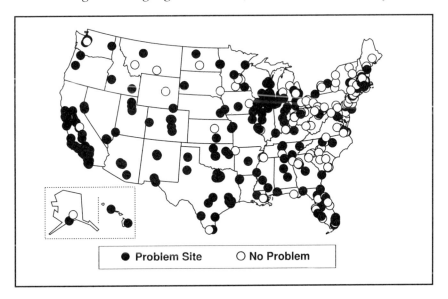

261 cities with gang crime problems by the end of 1991. In the following year, Klein extended his list of gang problem cities to "approximately 800." By 1995, Klein (p. 98) concluded that there were between 800 and 1,100 U.S. cities with gang crime problems and "more than 9,000 gangs and at least 400,000 gang members in any given year." Klein (p. 105) argued that the age of gang participation has not significantly declined over the years, but that the number of older members involved in gangs had increased particularly in cities with over a decade of problems. Gang members in the 800 gang problem cities identified by Klein remained predominantly African American and Latino/a, but he predicted a reduction in the proportion of Latino/a gang members associated with the proliferation of gangs in smaller cities.

The Institute for Intergovernmental Research, National Youth Gang Center Survey (1995)

In 1994, the Office of Juvenile Justice and Delinquency Prevention established the National Youth Gang Center (NYGC) in Tallahassee, Florida. In 1995, the NYGC conducted its first assessment of the national gang problem. A list of 4,120 localities from a variety of sources was compiled. Of the 3,440 responding agencies, 2,007 reported youth gang problems. This number consisted of 1,492 municipal police departments and 515 sheriffs' departments. As with the earlier surveys reviewed above, not all responding agencies could provide statistics on the magnitude of their local gang problem. In this survey 1,741 agencies reported a total of 23,388 youth gangs, and 1,499 agencies reported a total of 664,906 gang members. The numbers produced by the 1995 NYGC were larger than those of any prior one-year survey.

Trends in the Number of Gang Problem Jurisdictions

Since Miller's initial work, the number of jurisdictions reporting gang crime problems has steadily increased with each new and more comprehensive survey. Figure 1-7 presents this increase over time. To some extent, though, these statistics represent the increase in survey breadth as well as increased perception of the national-level scope of gang crime problems. In other words, the increasing numbers of gang crime cities identified by name in the national surveys from 1975 to 1996 reflected an increased perception of the spread of

Figure 1-7
Number of Cities With Gang Problems Identified by National Surveys

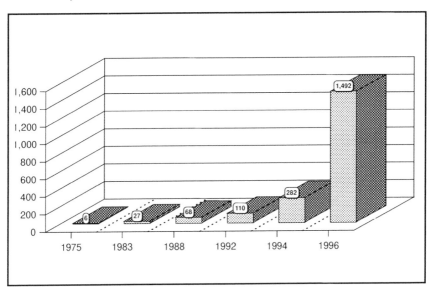

the gang problem by those planning surveys, as well as the changing perceptions of local officials. Likewise, the increase from the six gang cities that were identified in Miller's 1975 survey to the 1,492 gang cities and towns specifically identified by the 1995 National Youth Gang Center Survey and the 2,100 cities specifically identified by Miller (1997) as having reported a gang problem at any time in the 25 years constitutes a real expansion of the national gang crime problem as it is reported by local law enforcement agencies. For cities with populations between 25,000 and 150,000, between 1994 and 1995 three new cities per week saw the emergence of a gang problem.

Trends in the Number of Gangs

While most of the surveys have reported the number of gangs in the United States, we feel that it is a statistic that requires particular caution to interpret. The changing estimates from national surveys of the number of gangs are shown in Figure 1-8. In emerging gang problem cities where gangs are loosely organized, continual changes in the number of gangs are indicative of the collective and contagious nature of gang behavior (Decker and Van Winkle, 1994,

Figure 1-8
Number of Gangs Reported by National Surveys

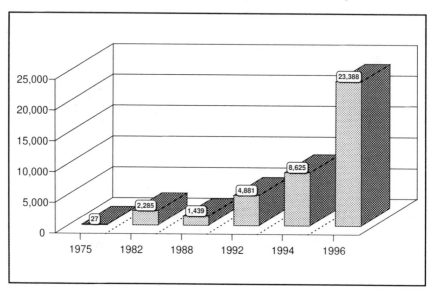

1996; Decker 1996); and, even in chronic gang problem cities such as Chicago, once powerful gangs such as the El Rukns can eventually become relatively unimportant parts of the local street gang problem (Toobin, 1994).

The Number of Gang Members

The number of gang members in the United States is doubly important. On one hand, it is a measure by law enforcement of the number of "at risk" youths whose lives have been touched by gang crime problems. The number of gang members reflects individual youths who either are or *potentially* are offenders or victims in gang-related violence. With alleged national increases in violence by juveniles, these numbers are suggestive of the role that gang organization may play in such increases and the associated costs for young lives. On the other hand, these numbers reflect the criminalization of large numbers of poor, predominantly minority youths. Figure 1-9 reflects changes in estimates of the numbers of gang members over 20 years of surveys of gang problems. Regardless of how the finding is interpreted, approximately half a million youths officially identified as gang members by police were reported by both the

Figure 1-9
Number of Gang Members Reported by National Surveys

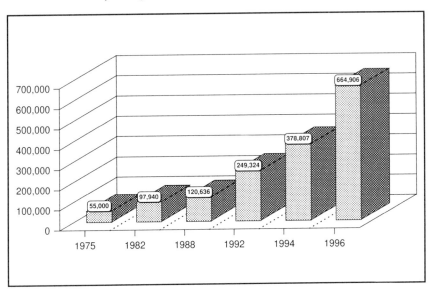

1994 NIJ Extended National Assessment survey and Malcolm Klein's national survey.

The Number of Gang-Related Crimes

The final statistic, the number of gang-related crimes, is the one that has been most neglected in law enforcement record keeping. The absence of estimates of gang crime from earlier surveys is predominantly a reflection of law enforcement policy rather than neglect by researchers. This statistic is the most important one for assessing the magnitude of gang crime problems at national and local levels. While "number of gangs" measures organizational changes that may have varying effects on the magnitude of gang crime and "number of members" may in part reflect criminal justice labeling, each counted gang-related crime reflects an actual violation of law that is associated with gang involvement. For violent and property crimes, each offense represents a victim or victims as well as an offender. As noted above, there must be careful control for variations in definition across jurisdictions and time in analyzing gang incident data, but it can be argued that the national conservative measure of 437,066 and the statistical estimate of 580,331 gang-related crimes for 1993 can be used as baseline data for future studies.

Summary of Key Points

There are a variety of definitions of gangs, a situation unlikely to change soon. However, most gang definitions include a group, its permanence, its use of symbols, and its involvement in crime. The efforts to count the number of gangs, gang members, and gang crimes have often been haphazard. Researchers found a lack of uniformity in the approach toward gangs taken by law enforcement departments. However, since the 1980s, a growing number of gang problem cities—and gangs and gang members—have been documented by a number of studies.

Chapter Two

The Link Between Gangs and Crime

Gang members participate in a large number of serious delinquent and criminal acts. What is not always clear is the role that gang membership plays in such acts. That is, many gang members commit crimes that have nothing to do with their membership. In this chapter we examine what is known about the relationship between gang membership on one hand and crime and delinquency on the other. First, we review information concerning the link between gangs and delinquency. Next, we place this information in the three contexts in which crime occurs: the individuals who join gangs, the gang itself as an organization, and the community in which gang activity takes place. Finally, we identify questions that need to be addressed to enhance our understanding of the relationship between crime and delinquency.

Gang Membership, Crime, and Delinquency

The distinction between gang-related crimes and crimes committed by gang members is important. Gang-related crimes are a function of gang membership or motivated by gang identification or goals. Crimes by gang members include gang-related crimes and crimes committed by individual gang members that have no relationship to gang membership or activity. We know that gang members are responsible for greater levels of crime and delinquency than their nongang counterparts. In addition, we know that gang-related delinquency is more violent than non-gang-related delinquency.

And, finally, we know that there is considerable variation across time, communities, and gangs in the scope and nature of gang-related crime and delinquency. We draw these three conclusions from field studies of gang activity, analyses of criminal justice data, and survey studies of gangs.

Field Studies

Without question, most of what we know about gangs has been learned from field studies. This methodology focuses on the nondelinquent and noncriminal aspects of gang behavior, as well as law-violating behavior, and is based on interviews with gang members, typically in their own neighborhoods. Here, we review what these studies tell us about the link between gangs and delinquency.

Table 2.1
Selected Field Research on Gangs
in the Twentieth Century United States

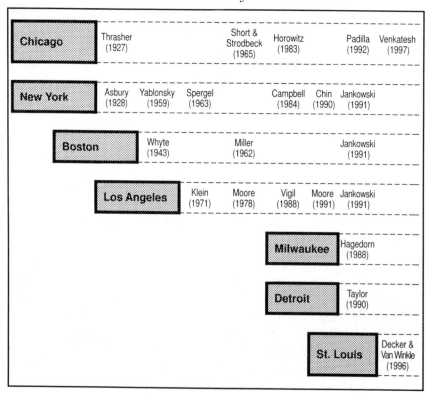

Asbury's Studies of New York City Gangs

Herbert Asbury (1928) studied gangs in the Five Points area of New York City, an area populated largely by recent Irish immigrants still mired in the economic underclass. He provided encyclopedic descriptions of the variety of gangs and their activities. The primary activities for these gangs were fighting, with each other as well as rival gangs. Asbury was careful to make the distinction between those who grew up in a gang and those criminals who organized to perform illegal acts more effectively. He described numerous small gangs with affiliations to a larger gang and suggested that most gang activity was concentrated in the neighborhoods among a small group of friends well-known to each other.

Thrasher's Study of Chicago Gangs

Frederic Thrasher's pioneering work appeared in 1927 and is the first serious academic treatment of gangs. In Thrasher's view, gangs originated from the spontaneous group activity of adolescents, strengthened by conflict over time. This process consisted of three stages. In its earliest stage, the gang was diffuse, it had little leadership, and it might have been short-lived. Some gangs progressed to the next stage, where they became solidified. Conflict with other gangs played a notable role in this process, helping to define group boundaries and strengthen the ties between members, uniting them in the face of threats from rivals. Thrasher (1927, pp. 116–117) pointed out, "The gang is a conflict group. It develops through strife and thrives on warfare. . . . In its struggle for existence a gang has to fight hostile groups to maintain its . . . privileges, its property rights, and the physical safety of its members." The endurance of the criminally involved gang in its social setting and the internal structure of the gang are, according to Thrasher, a product of continuing conflict that often resulted in intergang and intragang violence. The final step in the evolution of the gangs observed by Thrasher occurred when they became conventionalized and members assumed legitimate roles in society. For those groups that failed to make this transition, delinquent or criminal activity became the dominant focus of the group.

Activities within the gang, according to Thrasher, were diverse and motivated by typical youthful concerns, such as thrills and excitement. Gang members preyed on the community and stealing was the most common crime. Thrasher characterized many gangs as conflict groups that developed out of disputes and flourished in the presence of threats from rival groups. Fighting was the predominant activity, and fights with members of one's own gang were as likely as those with members of rival gangs. For gang members, violence served both to unite them and to speed the adaptation of the gang to its environment. In this way, violence played an especially important function in the integration of members into the group. The threat presented by rival gangs served to intensify the solidarity within the gang, especially for new members. Despite their involvement in criminal or delinquent activity, most gang members were also assimilated into legitimate social activities, most often athletics.

Whyte's Study of Boston Corner Boys

William Foote Whyte (1943) conducted a study of an older group of corner boys that he identified as the Nortons in depression-era Boston. The central unifying activity of the Nortons was an illegal gambling enterprise. The members had a history of collective participation in intergroup violence, though Whyte himself observed no violence. Whyte's study retains its importance because of its detailed descriptions of personal interaction among group members. It also provided a description of a group of Italian American young adults who were temporarily stalled in their life development by the Great Depression.

Yablonsky's Research on New York City Gangs

An important development in theory and research occurred with the appearance of Lewis Yablonsky's (1959, 1962) work on the violent gang. Drawing on Thrasher, he identified three types of gangs—delinquent gangs, violent gangs, and social gangs—indicating that the violent gang was the most persistent and problematic for society. Not unexpectedly, the role of violence looms large in every aspect of this gang. The violent gang forms in response to threats against safety, and thus represents a form of protection for its members. It has a loose structure and little formal character; for example, leaders in this type of gang change, and membership within gang subgroups in many cases is more important than the larger gang. Violence, the defining event for members of these types of gangs, can occur over seemingly senseless matters but most often in response to perceived threats against gang territory. Membership fulfills a number of needs; most importantly, it fulfills the psychological needs of boys incapable of finding such fulfillment in the larger society. Because of its lack of organization, Yablonsky identifies the violent gang as a "near group" (p. 272), with a "collective structure" situated somewhere between totally disorganized aggregates (like mobs) and well-organized aggregates (like delinquent or social gangs).

Spergel's Study of New York City Gangs

Irving Spergel (1964) observed and described in detail gangs in both Racketville and Slumtown. In Racketville, a predominantly Italian neighborhood, juveniles had better access to legitimate and illegitimate opportunity structures. Spergel (p. 65) described the Racketville gangs as primarily "defensive" in nature. To some extent, other community residents were willing to express their support of gang members in this role, especially so long as those defended against were minorities (p. 64). Ironically, the major conflicts were between two Italian-American youth gangs. Members of Racketville gangs were very likely to be lifelong friends (p. 71). Younger generations of gang members could identify influentials from earlier gang generations, and younger gang members respected older and former members of their gangs.

Gangs in the community that Spergel called Slumtown were drawn from populations of youths who had the least access to both legitimate and illegitimate opportunities that Spergel observed in his research. Based on both police records and interviews with gang members, Spergel (pp. 65–66) identified the gangs of this predominantly Puerto Rican neighborhood as "offensive" in nature and philosophy. He concluded that gang members in this community were above all else motivated by individual reputations and a desire for individual status defined in terms of toughness and fighting ability. Members of a particular gang were likely to know each other only by nickname and seldom knew older or former members of their gang or its history. In some cases, members would move from one gang to another, in order to enhance individual reputation by affiliating with a more successfully violent gang.

Short and Strodtbeck's Chicago Field Research

For three years, from 1959 to 1962, James F. Short and Fred L. Strodtbeck (1965) conducted a comparatively large research project around an evaluation of a detached street workers program administered by the YMCA of Metropolitan Chicago. The project contained both field observation and systematic survey components. The systematic survey and its results are discussed below. The field observation part of the project gathered detailed data on 16 gangs, 11 composed of African American members and five of whites. The gangs ranged in size of from 16 to 68 members. Short and Strodtbeck were particularly interested in how group and individual factors interacted to produce delinquent behavior. They found that when gang leaders perceived threats to their status as leaders within the gang, these leaders were more likely to engage in aggressive delinquent behavior or encourage it in others. For example, when gang leaders were incarcerated, new leaders might emerge to play the role in the gang that had previously belonged to the absent leader. In order to regain a lost leadership role, the returning leader would often display uncustomary levels of aggression. In another example, Short and Strodtbeck examined the contributions to male gang member status within the group that derived from fathering children outside of marriage.

The importance of the gang itself as a unit of analysis was highlighted by Short and Strodtbeck. They described how the community context, relationships among gang members, and the social characteristics of gang members influenced the degree to which gangs varied in their level of "conflict orientation." Two concepts central to their perspective on gangs were "threat" and "status." Short and Strodtbeck emphasized the importance of changes in patterns of organization within and between gangs over time. A particularly interesting observation was the way in which the assignment of a detached worker to a gang might serve as a collective recognition of status for the gang and result in reduced levels of violent delinquency (1965 p. 197). This suggestion posits a very different result from the one observed by Klein in Los Angeles which we examine next.

Klein's Research on Los Angeles Gangs

Malcolm Klein's (1971) study combined a theoretical approach to dealing with gangs with an action context of evaluating gang intervention programs. Two programs, the Group Guidance Project

(1961–65) and the Ladino Hills Project (1966–68) formed the basis of his analysis. Klein found that delinquency increased among gang members who received the most group-oriented services, and that solidarity among gang members seemed to increase as a result of the attention paid to the gang by street workers. This led Klein to the conclusion that gang intervention programs may have the un-expected result of contributing to the attractiveness of gangs, en-hancing their solidarity, and promoting more violence. He con-cluded that most characteristics of gang structure were difficult to differentiate from other features of adolescent street culture, and that gang members shared many common features with nongang adolescents. He concluded that gangs and gang members contained large variations within their respective ranks.

Klein's views of leadership and the sources of cohesion within gangs were consistent with his definition of gangs and gang mem-bership. In his view, leadership was largely age-related and was not so much a specific office as a mixture of functions. This reinforced the notion that gangs resembled the disorganized, spontaneous, and short-term features of youth culture more than they did formal adult structures. Further support for this contention was found in the consistent report by gang members that their primary activity was "hanging out" with other members on the street. Their delinquency was described as "cafeteria style" (p. 125) rather than a purposive, well-organized specialization. Cohesiveness, the force that keeps gangs together, was more a product of external sources than internal sources. That is, the bonds of gang membership do not become stronger in response to internal mechanisms (meetings, codes, signs, activities) but rather as a response to external pressures. The external sources of cohesion were structural (poverty, unemployment, and weak family socialization) but also included pressures that resulted from interaction with other gangs as well as members of one's own gang. In particular, the threat of violence from another gang in-creased solidarity within the gang, if it did not destroy the gang as an organization. As a consequence, most victims of gang violence were other gang members. Of particular concern to Klein was the role membership interaction played in strengthening gang cohe-siveness. The more gang members met and the more important their gang was perceived to be in the community, the stronger the bonds were between gang members. In general, Klein found that few gang goals existed outside of those generated by external pressures, and the few internal gang norms that did exist were weak and transient. Against this backdrop, Klein saw the intervention of detached workers and gang programs enhancing gang cohesiveness, making the dissolution of the gang a greater challenge.

The Ladino Hills Project gave Klein the opportunity to build on findings from the Group Guidance Project. A specific effort was made to avoid increasing gang solidarity, an outcome that would make the gang more attractive, increase membership, and expand delinquent activities. A working premise of this approach was that programmatic attention paid to gangs by such institutions as the police, social workers, and the schools had the unintended consequence of making the gang more attractive and should be avoided. Despite a decline in gang cohesiveness, the rate of delinquency increased, particularly for more serious crimes. However, the amount of delinquency overall declined, a decline that was concentrated among companionship offenses. The withdrawal of adults from gang activities diminished both gang cohesion and delinquency, important findings for both policy making and program direction and development.

Moore's Research on Los Angeles Gangs

Joan Moore (1978) has conducted the longest ongoing field research with gangs. Her work is the result of collaboration between academics, Chicano ex-convicts (referred to as Pintos), and gang members in the Mexican American neighborhoods of East Los Angeles. Moore places primary importance on the role of Chicano culture and the position of Mexican Americans within the cultural and institutional life of East Los Angeles in explaining gang formation and activities. Her work underscored the isolation of the barrio from mainstream life in Los Angeles, particularly its political and economic detachment. In her earlier work (1978), gangs from three barrios (White Fence, Hoyo Maravilla, and San Fernando) were studied through the use of Pintos as research associates.

Moore and her associates isolated three distinctive characteristics of Chicano gangs: (1) they were territorially based, (2) they had a strong age-graded structure resulting in "klikas" or cohort groups, and (3) fighting occupied a central role in Chicano gang life. After fighting, drugs played a prominent role in the life of gangs.

Contrary to Klein's earlier findings, Moore emphasized the lifelong role that gangs played for their members and communities. Adult gang members were numerous, and played a role in the intergenerational transmission of gang membership within neighborhoods. The strong ethnic culture of Chicanos also helped to shape the structure and activities of Chicano gangs. In part, this occurred as a result of the high rate of imprisonment of Chicano gang members. In prison, ethnic gangs attracted and socialized inmates from their neighborhood who had not previously been involved in gang activity. Thus, a prison gang culture was formed that ultimately found a role on the street. Moore argued that the continuities between Chicano prison gangs and those on the street are strong because the experiences in the prison and neighborhood are similar. That is, Chicanos are not included in the mainstream of the economy or political structure in either setting. This enhances ethnic solidarity and produces the pressures that cause increased cohesion among gang members.

Field researchers rarely get the opportunity to return to their subjects and setting years after an initial analysis, yet such a procedure is essential for documenting changes over time. Moore (1991) accomplished this by returning to two of the neighborhoods she studied earlier, White Fence and Hoyo Maravilla. She was able to develop a list of gang members from her earlier work, from which a random sample of 156 men and women were chosen for in-depth interviews. Her findings underscored the effect that the growth of the urban underclass has had on gangs and their activities. In addition to the evaporation of many employment opportunities, the decline of housing, poor schools, and dramatic population changes (movement of the middle and working classes from traditional neighborhoods) created conditions that altered the nature of the barrio and its gangs.

Early gangs began as "friendship groups" (p. 31) that had informal structures, and claimed a territory as their own. Members were committed to protecting themselves and their neighborhood. These gangs had a strong age-graded structure; cliques within the gang of boys and girls of the same age were the primary source of gang activity. Over time, gangs became more institutionalized in their neighborhoods and exerted greater influence over the lives of their members. This was a consequence of the growth of the underclass.

In addition, gangs neutralized the socialization power of other institutions in the neighborhood, enhancing their ability to grow stronger.

Reflecting their territorial nature, most gang members came from the same neighborhood. There was little evidence that adolescents were forced into joining the gang; rather, it was a normal outcome of hanging out with a certain group of friends. Gang members spent most of their time hanging around the neighborhood. The major change in gangs from the 1950s to the present was the increase in aggression. There was not much evidence that gang members had defective personalities or disproportionately came from families with problems. Moore found that having a productive job was the single most important strategy for being successful in the barrio.

Horowitz's Research on a Chicago Gang

Ruth Horowitz (1983) studied a gang in a Chicano community in Chicago—the Lions—and, situated her analysis of gangs and gang members in the context of Latino/a culture and the marginality of ethnic groups from the larger culture. She observed them in the early 1970s and again in the late 1970s, as members of the Lions made the transition from teenagers to adults. Her analysis focused on the often competing demands for honor made by local culture and the expectations of the American Dream that emanated from the dominant culture. The subculture of the gang represented one solution to the demands of honor, demands that placed a high premium on self-respect and character, both individual characteristics. Despite the allegiance to these values, the American Dream, emphasizing educational attainment and work, had a powerful sway over these young men and women.

The Lions had existed on 32nd Street since the 1950s, and membership was comprised primarily of male Chicano residents and had a considerable presence on the streets of the neighborhood. Most young men joined the gang at some point in their lives, though typically for only a short time. Members were between 12 and 17 years of age, and strong age-grading existed within the gang. Approximately 15 to 40 members belonged to each age grouping. While there were some rules of membership and a vague leadership structure, Horowitz characterized the gang as having considerable flexibility. Despite this, she observed collective goals, different roles, and membership stability. Violence was a regular feature of gang life, and members had to be prepared to respond to assailants at any time. Horowitz noted that gang members armed themselves in the belief that their rivals had guns; they sought to increase the sophistication of their weaponry in the hopes that they won't be "left short," that is, caught in a shootout with less firepower than their rivals. Despite many maturational pressures and opportunities to leave the gang, a number of members remained into their early 20s.

Campbell's Research on Female Gang Members

Ann Campbell (1984) conducted field work with three female gangs in New York City. She spent six months with each of three different types of female gangs: (1) a street gang, (2) a biker gang, and (3) a "religio-cultural" gang. By focusing on one girl in each gang, she provided a study more akin to the life histories that Shaw and McKay wrote in the 1920s. Campbell argued that female gangs and their members could only be understood against the backdrop of their life conditions as young women in poor neighborhoods. Her work calls into question the stereotypical portrayal of female gang members as either "marginal" members of society, or "parasitical" attachments to male gangs. While noting that these characterizations could be applied accurately to a large number of female gangs, the diversity of female gangs prohibited their blanket acceptance.

Campbell identified the two predominant roles that female gang members play—sex objects or tomboys. Sex objects are viewed in a proprietary fashion by male gang members, and females in this role were submissive to the will of male gang members. Such females often were marginal gang members and could not form a gang separate from the male gang. Tomboys, however engaged in more typically "male" gang activities such as fighting, committing crimes, and "hanging out." In each of the three female gangs she observed, Campbell found some evidence of leadership roles and gang structure, though typically less than in the male gangs they were affiliated with. The girls in Campbell's gangs had a much larger life outside the gang than did their male counterparts, primarily because of their familial responsibilities. The duties of housekeeping, babysitting younger brothers and sisters, and rearing one's own children fell disproportionately on the shoulders of female gang members. In a sense, these responsibilities insulated them from further gang involvement. Campbell's work found that female gangs seldom operated beyond the shadow of a male gang.

Vigil's Research on Barrio Gangs

James Diego Vigil (1988), who worked with Moore and the Pinto project from 1976 through 1978, spent three years in the field compiling 67 life histories of gang members in Los Angeles. Like Moore, he emphasized the unique nature of Chicano culture in the formation of gangs. In particular, he identified "choloization," the process by which Chicano youth are "marginalized" from mainstream society. From Vigil's perspective, Chicano youth are in a position of multiple marginality, that is, they are marginal to several aspects of mainstream culture and institutional life. The street provides an alternative socialization path for these youths, most of whom are excluded from participation in mainstream institutional activities and lack families capable of providing alternatives to street socialization. Because gang members share many negative experiences in common—family stress, school failure, and lack of interest in legitimate activities—the gang provides a collective solution to the problem of identity.

Chicano gangs are comprised primarily of males between the ages of 13 and 25 for whom neighborhood identification is strong. Most members start in the gang at a young age. Gangs ranged in size from 10 to 100, though the average size was 36. The primary reason for joining was to be with one's friends, though direct physical confrontations propelled some youths into gangs. While an age-graded structure was present, little formal hierarchy and rule structure was observed by Vigil. Violence was a constant feature of gang life, though it was threatened more often than it occurred.

Hagedorn's Research on Milwaukee Gangs

The growth of the urban underclass has been linked to an increase in gangs (Jackson, 1991). Research supporting this perspective finds its most outspoken advocate in the work of John Hagedorn (1988), and is supported by Pamela Jackson (1991). Hagedorn interviewed 47 gang members who were the founders of 19 of Milwaukee's largest gangs. He argued that local economic and demographic factors were the most important variables in explaining the emergence and nature of gangs. Hagedorn is especially interested in explaining the origins of gangs. He observed that many Milwaukee gangs took the names used by gangs in Chicago, but there was little evidence that gangs from Chicago had come to Milwaukee to form "satellites." Rather, most gangs in his city emerged on a more or less spontaneous basis from "corner groups," young men who hung out together in their neighborhoods. Others emerged from "dancing" groups that experienced physical threats and fighting, strengthening their alliances and ultimately resulting in gang formation.

Many similarities exist between the gangs studied by Thrasher in 1920s Chicago and by Short and Strodtbeck in Chicago in the 1960s and those described by Hagedorn. One difference was that, like Moore, he found that gangs were not strictly comprised of adolescents; rather, they underwent a "natural splintering process" (p. 5) as gang members aged and moved into different roles within the gangs. Gangs exhibited little formal organization, had few roles or responsibilities, and their activities were more likely to originate from subsets within the gang than from the entire gang acting as a unit. Crime was a small part of the overall activities gang members engaged in; like their nongang adolescent counterparts, hanging out, partying, and sports occupied most of a gang member's time. For Hagedorn, the gang served as a family-like organization, and in many cases provided a means of survival. Traditional social controls had a weak effect on the behavior of gang members, in part because gang members were isolated from mainstream society. While gang members sold drugs, drug sales were not well organized and provided only a modest level of income. Violence was an integral part of life in the gang, and gang members were expected to use violence against rival gang members.

Chin's Research on New York City Asian American Gangs

Ko-lin Chin (1990) provided a unique in-depth study of Asian American gangs. Chin framed his analysis of these contemporary gangs in a detailed history of the traditions and structures of Chinese societies, such as the triads. These traditions and belief systems provide a cultural mythology that can be used to motivate gang member loyalty and discipline and convince victims of the inevitability of their exploitation. Still, Chin referred to the gangs that he studied as "non-traditional crime groups" in the subtitle of his book. Gang

members had limited knowledge and commitment to Asian traditions. While gang members ran criminal networks with the extortion
of Asian American legitimate and illegitimate businesses as their
targets, the victimization and the victimizing represented a dynamic
that capitalized on the marginalization of Asian Americans in U.S.
society and extreme levels of gang violence. One process that drove
the patterns of gang organization and violence in New York City
was the recurring waves of Asian migration, enculturation, and exploitation. The traditions that Chin described are essentially Chinese; the participants in Asian American gang violence were Korean
and Southeast Asian, as well as Chinese.

Chin (1990) observed that in some years, violence between gangs
gave way to periods dominated by intragang violence. It may be
possible that increases in intragang violence are associated with the
patterns of "war and peace" that Thrasher felt characterize the life
history of the gang. In the examples Chin described (pp. 86–88),
increases in intragang violence appear to be associated with the
gangs' achieving a level of stability in terms of securing their territories for profit-making criminal activity and their places in the social structure of the greater community.

Taylor's Research on Detroit African-American Gangs

Carl Taylor (1990) studied a variety of gangs with shifting membership and structures over time. From his findings Taylor constructed an ordered typology of Detroit gangs. Scavenger gangs
were extremely loosely organized. Leadership and structure
changed on an almost daily basis in these gangs. Among scavenger
gangs, delinquency was "senselessly" violent and generally spontaneous and unplanned. Territory, either geographic or defined in
terms of criminal markets, served as the organizational cement that
held what Taylor identified as territorial gangs together. Goals, prof-
itable enterprises, and leadership—all emerged as territorial gangs
developed. Taylor also found corporate gangs that he considered
highly organized with collectively established criminal agendas.
Violence by corporate gangs was systematic and could be rationally
associated with criminal gain by the gang. All of the gangs studied
by Taylor engaged in crime and delinquency. Each time a gang became more organized there was an increase in violence.

Sanchez-Jankowski's Research on Gangs in Three Cities

The work of Martin Sanchez-Jankowski (1991) was among the more ambitious field studies of gangs. Over a 10-year period, he conducted an ethnographic study of gangs in New York, Boston, and Los Angeles. During this time, he was a participant-observer of 37 randomly selected gangs representing multiple ethnic groups (including Chicano, Dominican, Puerto Rican, Central American, African American, and Irish). His work provides a radically different view of gangs than his predecessors. He described gang members as "defiant individualists" who possessed several distinctive character traits including competitiveness, wariness, self-reliance, social isolation, strong survival instincts, and a "social Darwinist view of the world." Despite this, he viewed gangs as "formal-rational" organizations, having strong organizational structures, well-defined roles, rules that guided member activities, penalties for rule violations, an ideology, and well-defined means for generating both legal and illegal income. Sanchez-Jankowski observed that gangs function much like private governments and argued that many gangs have positive relationships with people in their neighborhoods, often performing essential functions such as looking out for the well-being of the community in which they live. Much like local patriots, all of the gangs he studied attempted to develop ties to organized crime syndicates in their city. For Sanchez-Jankowski gang crime is purposive and well organized.

Padilla's Study of a Chicago Drug-Selling Gang

Felix Padilla (1992) spent over a year studying the "Diamonds," a Puerto Rican youth gang in Chicago. Gang members were second-generation immigrants contacted through social service agencies and "key informants." The gang was predominantly an "ethnic enterprise" (p. 3) involved in street drug sales. Adopting the approach chosen by Moore and Vigil, Padilla attempted to understand the gang by focusing on the ethnic experiences of Puerto Rican youth in Anglo culture. Critical to this perspective was the view that these individuals experienced cultural rejection and as a consequence found little hope in its social institutions.

Despite their active involvement in street drug dealing, the primary gang activity was "hanging out;" playing basketball and attending parties comprised two of the other major ways gang members spent their time. Hanging out played an important role in the gang because it represented the way that gang members "marked" their turf and protected it from infringement from rival gangs attempting to "move in" on the Diamonds' turf. Violence played an important role in the first gang activity (initiation) and an important symbolic role in gang life. Violence communicates a message to gang members and nongang members alike and is a regular part of life in the gang. Violence also serves to reinforce the solidarity among gang members and accentuate the boundaries between gang and nongang members. Interestingly, being labeled as a gang member by a rival gang led other boys to join the gang. In this way, they joined the gang "out of necessity," seeking the protection of their neighborhood gang from gangs in rival neighborhoods.

Drug dealing was the primary criminal activity of the gang, and many gang members referred to it as "work" in the same way they referred to legitimate jobs. However, street drug sales varied in many ways. There was considerable variation in the types of drugs sold, how they were sold, the uses for drug profits, and the roles involved in drug sales. Large amounts of capital were seldom accumulated; rather, the proceeds most often went toward more typical adolescent pursuits such as partying, food, clothes, and dating. The gang was a good vehicle for street drug sales because the collectivism generated by the gang worked for the business side of drug dealing. Unlike the gangs described by Klein and by Short and Strodtbeck, there were clear roles in drug selling and a clear organizational structure. "Pee Wees," 13- to 15-year-olds, demonstrated their cunning and willingness to take risks by stealing. If successful, they could become runners or "mules" who moved drugs by the time they reached the age of 16. The most successful runners sold drugs directly on the streets. For Padilla's gang members, these represented sequential steps in the career development of gang members.

Decker's Research on St. Louis Gangs

A comprehensive study of gang crime in St. Louis was conducted by Scott Decker and his colleagues with support from the Family Youth Service Bureau, U.S. Department of Health and Human Services (Decker and Van Winkle 1994, 1996; Decker 1996). Decker and his team of researchers followed Hagedorn's (1990) dictum that the most effective method to gain information about active gang members is to contact the gang members themselves in their natural environment, the streets and neighborhoods where they live. With the assistance of a street ethnographer (a community resident and former participant in St. Louis street life) in-depth interviews with 99 gang members, 24 relatives, and 28 ex-gang members were used to construct a portrait of the violent and dynamic social world of St. Louis gangs. From the St. Louis gang project, an image emerged of gang structures and processes that presented a unique combination of local neighborhood dynamics and what Klein (1995, p. 230) has identified as the national-level diffusion of gang cultures. St. Louis neighborhood rivalries dating back for decades and contemporary friendship networks were transfigured into a system of conflict structures that bear the names and symbols of California's long-standing conflict between the Bloods and Crips (Jackson and McBride, 1986; Covey, Menard, Franzere, 1992) with occasional symbolic manifestations of Chicago gang culture. Information produced by the project represented the beliefs and practices of 29 gangs (16 affiliated with the Crips cultural identification and 13 affiliated with Bloods contingents).

From a survey of members of a politically appointed gang task force, members of a police juvenile squad, and a population of juvenile detainees, Decker and Leonard (1991) documented the divergence in perspective on the magnitude and nature of the gang crime problem in St. Louis. From their interviews with gang members, Decker and Van Winkle (1994, 1996; Decker 1996) found that gang members in St. Louis were frequently involved in the sale of drugs, but such sales were seldom well organized and almost never a manifestation of gang organization. Above all, gang life in St. Louis was ubiquitously integrated into a socially organized and culturally grounded pattern of violence. Decker (1996) portrayed a St. Louis gang problem that was characterized and defined by violence. Violence determined the community-level emergence and development of gangs in St. Louis. Violence also defined the day-to-day substance and meaning of gang activity in St. Louis. When St. Louis gang members were asked how their particular gangs could be reformed or dispersed, they were most likely to proclaim violence as the only antidote to the violent activity and philosophy that defined their gang's existence. Because their membership posed a threat to family members, schools, neighbors, and social institutions, Decker suggested that the violence that dominated gang behavior among St. Louis gangs increased gang member marginalization. Therefore, efforts to reduce gang violence have important policy consequences for reintegrating gang youth into mainstream social institutions.

Venkatesh's Ethnography of Gangs in Chicago Public Housing

As a graduate research assistant, Sudhi Venkatesh was assigned to administer a formal social survey instrument to residents of a Chicago community. His chance meeting with gang members became his gateway to a four-year participant-observation study of the relationships between a street gang and the residents of a public housing complex that he referred to as "Blackstone." In addition to the gang, organizational actors in the social life of the housing project included the project's elected citizens' council, a social service agency, the housing authority administration, and law enforcement. During his study, Venkatesh recorded the social processes that ensued when the gang leaders attempted to transform their gang from a conflict-oriented group striving to defend turf and symbols into a "corporate" entity with economic and social goals linked to those of the community. This process of "corporatism" as observed by Venkatesh included the consolidation and stabilization of drug-trafficking operations and the transfer of revenues from these illicit activities into a role in the day-to-day life of community residents. Though direct cash transfers to community leaders were involved, the central efforts in the gang's attempt to integrate itself into the Blackstone community included loans to residents, posting bail bonds, free groceries and clothing to needy residents, and the organization of recreational activities, as well as a professed commitment to social order and safety. In return, gang members received varying levels of noninterference with and support for their illegal activity as well as residents' failure to cooperate with law enforcement efforts to drive gang members from the housing project. Ultimately Venkatesh concluded that the gang's effort to become integrated into the community for any long-term basis failed as a result of the decline in revenues associated with the collapse of the gang's drug-trafficking enterprise.

Studies of Criminal Justice Data

Where field studies have provided broad images of delinquent and nondelinquent behavior by gang members, analyses of criminal justice data and systematic survey designs focus on specific features of gang member involvement in crime and delinquency. Field studies, to some extent, provide an effort to understand gang involvement from the perspective of the gang members themselves. Analyses of criminal justice data and systematic survey designs constitute approaches that analyze and categorize the behavior of gang members in terms that are of interest to nongang members.

National Surveys

Much of what we know of criminal justice system data on gang-related crime and delinquency stems from a series of national-level surveys of law enforcement and other agencies regarding gang crime problems. Reviewed in Chapter 1, these surveys were conducted by Miller, Needle, Stapleton, Spergel, Curry, Klein, the National Youth Gang Center, and others. On one hand, these surveys have drawn criticism for relying on law enforcement records, especially from those who have been concerned that the contemporary reaction to gangs constitutes a moral panic. On the other hand, these projects have demonstrated the magnitude of national-level concern with gangs as a crime problem.

Analyses of Los Angeles Criminal Justice Data

Maxson, Klein, and Cunningham (1992, p. 1) stress the utility of analyzing criminal justice data for understanding gang-related crime and delinquency: "With the number of cities having documented street gang problems swelling to well over 200, law enforcement is currently the best source available for comparisons of gang prevalence and violence." Cheryl Maxson and Malcolm Klein, with other colleagues, have supported their contention by producing a decade of research results from the systematic analysis of law enforcement data from agencies in the Los Angeles area. Maxson, Gordon, and Klein (1985) examined Los Angeles police and sheriff's department records on over 700 homicides to show that significant differences in social characteristics exist between gang and nongang homicides. Gang homicides were more likely to involve minority males, automobiles, public places, firearms, and a greater number of participants. The gang homicides were predominantly intra-ethnic in nature. Gang homicides were likely to involve perpetrators and victims with no prior personal contact and were characterized by a "relative absence of 'innocent bystander' victims" (p. 219). While gang homicide perpetrators and victims were significantly younger than their counterparts involved in nongang homicides, they were older than the "typical" youth gang member. In an extension of their analyses of homicide, Klein and Maxson (1989, p. 223) found that fear of retaliation was three times more likely to be characteristic of gang homicides than other homicides involving juveniles. By applying the Chicago motive-based definition to Los Angeles homicide data, Maxson and Klein (1990) showed that official estimates of gang-related homicides can vary dramatically across jurisdictions simply as a function of official definition. The potential for comparing the social structure of gang violence across communities was stressed in another effort (Maxson, Klein, and Gordon, 1990) that emphasized variations in the structure of gang violence across time and jurisdictions.

Klein, Maxson, and Cunningham (1991) used police arrest records from five Los Angeles area police stations to examine the differences between crack sales involving gang members and those involving nongang members. They were interested in several specific hypotheses, particularly that crack increased the control of drug markets by gangs, and increases in violence were linked to the disproportionate involvement of gang members in crack sales. They found no support for either of these contentions and argued that each was based on an incorrect view of gang organization and social structure. Central to their concerns were the consistent lack of an effective organizational structure within gangs, absence of permanent membership or roles, and the lack of shared goals. Compared to nongang transactions, gang crack sales were more likely to occur on the street, involve firearms, include younger suspects, and disproportionately involve African Americans suspects. However, most of these differences were small. Klein and his coauthors concluded by noting that gang membership added little of a distinctive nature to street drug sales, and while the problems associated with gangs and drug sales intersected, they were not a single problem (1991, p. 635).

Extending the analysis of drug arrest data to two Los Angeles suburban cities for 1989 to 1991, Maxson (1995) found that gang members were more likely to be involved in cocaine arrests. Gang members were involved in 27 percent of cocaine sales arrests, but less than 12 percent of arrests for selling other drugs. Arrests of gang members were more likely to involve rock or crack cocaine, males, African American offenders, and younger offenders.

Analyses of Chicago Criminal Justice Data

By studying the characteristics of the participants in gang and nongang homicides in Chicago, Spergel (1984) identified a number of social characteristics that distinguished gang offenders from nongang offenders. Using census, criminal justice, and social agency data, Curry and Spergel (1988) studied the distribution of gang homicide rates (as recorded by the Chicago Police Department) across community areas and time. They found that social variables, particularly ethnic composition and poverty were significantly related to differences in homicide rates across areas and time. Carolyn and Richard Block (1993) have used the Chicago incident data to study patterns of lethal and nonlethal gang-related violence over time. Block and Block used a Geographic Information System (GIS) method of clustering crime locations into "hot spots." The identification of such hot spots can greatly enhance police flexibility in tactically responding to gang violence. Among their findings, Block and Block showed that (1) gang violence is more likely to be turf-related than drug-related; (2) differences were observed in the patterns of violence of the four largest established street gangs and smaller, less-established gangs; and (3) guns were the lethal weapons in practically all Chicago gang-related homicides between 1987 and 1990.

Other Analyses of Criminal Justice Data on Gangs

Maxson and Klein (1994) have completed a national-level survey of law enforcement agencies about the nature of street gang migration. Based on interviews with police officials in over 1,000 jurisdictions, they identified over 700 cities with perceived gang migration problems. From these jurisdictions, Maxson and Klein selected 263 sites to be the target of more in-depth interviews. Case studies were also conducted in three jurisdictions. According to law enforcement respondents, social factors including family ties are the primary motivation for the migration of individual members, and most gang members move from city to city as individuals rather than in groups. Not all analyses of law enforcement information have employed complex quantitative methodology. William Sanders (1994) used observations of police performance and interviews with law enforcement and with incarcerated gang members to develop a grounded theoretical analysis of gang-related crime in San Diego. The transition over a 10-year period from less violent and fatal "gangbangs" to more fatal "drivebys" was his central finding.

Survey Studies of Gangs

In his overview of gang research, Irving Spergel (1990, p. 287) asserted, "The relationship between gangs and violence is most evident when patterns of behavior by gang members and nonmembers are compared. Gang youths engage in more crime of a violent nature than do nongang but delinquent youths." This comparison is best understood by systematic surveys that compare the delinquent behavior of gang and nongang youths.

Short and Strodtbeck's Chicago Survey

James Short and Fred Strodtbeck (1965) conducted an interview schedule explicitly designed to test Cohen's (1955) subculture theory, Miller's (1958) lower class-culture theory, and Cloward and Ohlin's (1960) theory of differential opportunity. With this instrument, they surveyed six subpopulations of male youths: middle-class African Americans, lower-class African Americans, African American gang members, middle-class whites, lower-class whites, and white gang members. While they found limited support for all three theoretical perspectives, Short and Strodtbeck identified a "conflict factor" among gang members that was defined by individual fighting, group fighting, carrying concealed weapons, and assault.

Fagan's Surveys in Three Cities

Jeffrey Fagan (1989, 1990) constructed cluster samples of 500 high school students and snowball samples of 50 high school dropouts from each of three cities: Chicago, Los Angeles, and San Diego.

Each sample was predominantly African American and Latino/a, and mixed in terms of gender. Gang membership was measured by self-report. He found that gang members committed more delinquent acts than did nongang members. Overall, Fagan concluded that gang members, male and female, had more serious delinquent involvement than nongang youths.

Spergel and Curry's Chicago Socialization to Gangs Survey

The baseline data of the Socialization to Gangs (STG) study was constructed in 1987 by surveying all male students in the sixth through eighth grades at four middle schools from a low-income neighborhood in the near northwest area of Chicago (Spergel and Curry, 1989). The communities surrounding the selected schools were marked by disproportionate numbers of gang homicides in Chicago's police records. Curry and Spergel (1992) found that the two ethnic subpopulations, Latino/a and African American, varied in terms of what factors were most likely to predict gang involvement. Latino/a gang involvement was more likely to be associated with social and psychological variables concerned with school and peer groups, while African American gang involvement was more associated with exposure to gang members. By analyzing longitudinal police data on the STG population over the five years following the initial survey, Curry (1994) demonstrated that the study population was indeed at "extreme risk" for serious gang related crime. In addition to early adolescent gang involvement, school and family-linked variables exhibited independent relationships to subsequent officially measured criminal gang involvement. As with other research, the number of offenses attributed to gang delinquents in the study population far exceeded those attributed to nongang delinquents. Gang members committed 2.7 times as many offenses as the nongang members of the population.

Esbensen and Colleagues' Analyses of the Denver Youth Survey

Finn-Aage Esbensen and his co-authors (Esbensen, Huizinga, and Weiher, 1993; Esbensen and Huizinga, 1993) used a longitudinal survey of an at-risk youth population in Denver to identify factors that differentiate gang and nongang youths, the involvement of gang members in delinquent activity, and the relationship between criminal offenses and gang membership. Gang membership was measured by respondent self-report. The researchers found that gang members do not differ from other youth involved in serious street-level offenses on factors such as commitment to delinquent peers and commitment to positive peers. While gang membership was rare among the Denver respondents, Esbensen and Huizinga (1993) found that gang members reported two or three times as much delinquency as nongang members. When gang members in the Denver study were asked what kinds of activities their gangs were involved in, fighting with other gangs was the most frequently reported behavior.

Analyses of the Rochester Youth Development Study

From longitudinal survey results on a representative sample of Rochester youth, Terrence Thornberry and his colleagues (1993) found that gang-involved youths were significantly more likely to report involvement in violence and other delinquency. By following youths over time, their analysis showed gang involvement to be a transitional process with delinquent activity increasing during gang involvement and declining afterward. Beth Bjerregaard and Carolyn Smith (1993), also using the Rochester data set, systematically examined gender differences in gang involvement. They found surprisingly little difference in the factors that explained male and female gang involvement. Increased involvement in delinquency and substance abuse were observed in both male and female gang members. The only major difference observed was that failure in school was more important for understanding female gang involvement.

Understanding Gang Involvement in Crime and Delinquency

Gang crime and delinquency involve three levels of inquiry, as illustrated in Figure 2-1: individual, gang, and community. Key questions about understanding gang involvement in crime and delinquency are: (1) Do individuals who join gangs differ from individuals who do not? (2) What are the social mechanisms about gangs that facilitate involvement in crime and delinquency? In particular, what are the positive factors that pull people toward their gang? (3) To what degree is gang crime a consequence of community-level factors? There are a number of factors, such as being in the under-

Figure 2-1
Levels of Explanation in Gang Delinquency

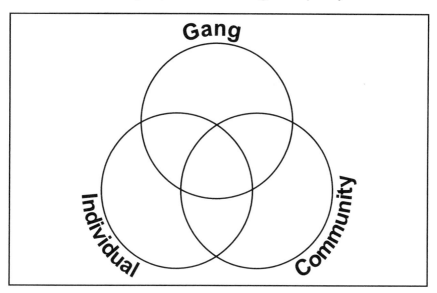

class, that help push young people into gangs. Finally, we must understand how these levels of inquiry interact with each other. For example, how do individual gang member characteristics and variations in gang structure interact with community forces?

Individual-Level Explanations of Gang Membership

Most of our understanding of gangs comes from sociologists and criminologists who study the group context of gang membership. After all, it is the aggregations of individuals—the gang—that we are most interested in. Yet, several commentators have focused on the characteristics of the individuals who join the gang and participate in gang activities.

The earliest effort to characterize individual gang members is Lewis Yablonsky's (1970) typology of gangs. Yablonsky, involved in the study of therapeutic communities, observed three types of gangs: (1) the delinquent gang, (2) the violent gang, and (3) the social gang. The violent gang was of greatest interest to Yablonsky. It was dominated by individuals who had sociopathic personalities. Such individuals in Yablonsky's scheme were incapable of remorse and unable to empathize with others. As a consequence, these gang members engaged in violence as a means to enhance their prestige or status among gang members or simply for "kicks." Violent gangs serve as outlets for satisfying emotional urges that focus on individual psychological needs. Yablonsky identified such individuals as acting out their personal problems, such as inadequacy, by engaging in gang violence. Typically, such individuals feel inadequate without their gang, and the gang provides psychic fulfillment otherwise missing in their lives.

Other commentators have pointed to the role that the gang plays in fulfilling psychological needs. For example, psychologists such as Arnold Goldstein (1991) describe the psychic needs fulfilled by gang membership. Gangs attract individuals with similar personality backgrounds and psychological needs. Jack Katz (1988) and Martin Sanchez-Jankowski (1991) each underscores the role of individual personality types in gangs. For Sanchez-Jankowski, gang members tend to be "defiant individualists," persons driven by the need to reduce external controls (from schools, parents, and the law) over their behavior. As a consequence, they are naturally resistant to authority. And for Katz, gang members engage in behaviors designed to create dread among rival gang members and other neighbors. They do so to fulfill psychic needs for dominating individuals and social settings.

Despite their occasional popularity, psychological approaches to understanding gangs and gang members are ultimately destined to fail. Such approaches ignore the most essential element of the gang, its group character.

It is possible that gangs attract individuals already heavily involved in criminal behavior. In this case, gang membership itself would contribute little to the increased levels of crime and delinquency observed among gang members. Without longitudinal data and information on comparable control youths, this possibility is difficult to establish. For Sanchez-Jankowski (1991, p. 23), the defining feature of gang membership is the development of a "defiant individualist character." By "character," he refers to "a group of personal traits structured in such a manner as to constitute a psychological system." An alternative perspective emerges from Taylor's description of scavenger gang members that he studied. Taylor (1990, p. 4) noted, "Members generally have the characteristics of being low achievers and illiterates with short attention spans who are prone to violent, erratic behavior." Spergel (1995, p. 163) uses the term *personal disorganization* to describe an individual-level vulnerability to gang involvement. Personal disorganization consists of limitations in intellectual and personality development and in self-control. For Spergel (p. 168), "The gang youth is not so much a deviant or a rebel, attached to a set of different, deviant, or criminal norms and values and relationships, as he or she is unattached to criminal or conventional systems. He seeks a closer, more adequate connection, but does not know how, where, or when to establish such a connection. The gang represents for him an available structure of social attachment and connection during a period of adolescent identity crisis."

The Gang

Gang membership plays a substantial role in increasing the level of criminal and delinquent behavior. The group context of gang behavior may provide support and opportunities for its members to engage in both more illegal behavior as well as more serious illegal behavior. (This is not to assume that organizational factors outside the gang are operative in the shaping of gang phenomena. We choose to view the organizational influences of schools, law enforcement, and even the families of gang members as elements of the community context of gang delinquency.) Esbensen, Huizinga, and Weiher (1993) found that gang members do not differ from other street-level offenders on a number of social psychological measures, yet their level of offending is greater. Thornberry et al. (1993, p. 175) outlined three alternative explanations of gang delinquency: (1) the "kind of person" model, (2) the social facilitation (or "kind of group") model, and (3) the enhancement (or interaction of person and group) model. To choose among these three models, Thornberry and his colleagues argued that two hypotheses must be tested. First, differences in delinquency between gang members and nongang members must be studied. Second, comparisons across individuals and individual careers must be made before, during, and after gang membership. Based on their longitudinal data, Thornberry and his colleagues found the strongest support for the social facilitation model. Performing a comparable analysis on their Denver data, Esbensen and Huizinga (1993, p. 583) reached a similar conclusion, "Our findings . . . lead us to conclude that it is not solely individual characteristics

Figure 2-2
The Collective Behavior Process of Gang Violence, Decker (1993)

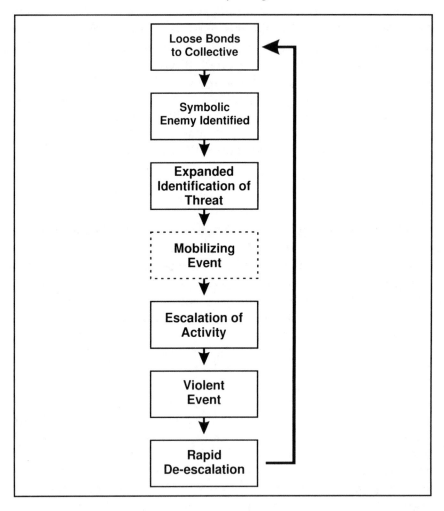

that are associated with higher levels of involvement in street crime. Rather, there may well be factors within the gang milieu that contribute to the criminal behavior of gang members."

Decker (1996) suggested that the growth in gangs and gang violence can be described by what Colin Loftin (1984) has called "contagion." In this context, contagion refers to subsequent acts of violence caused by an initial act; such acts typically take the form of

Figure 2-3
Multiple Level of Gang Delinquency (Decker & Van Winkle, 1996)

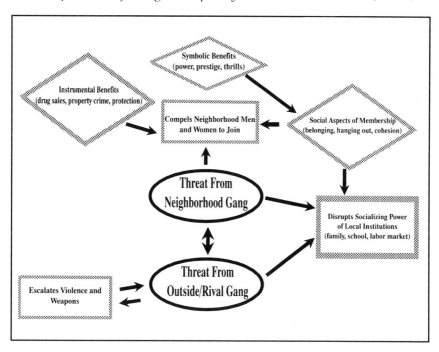

retaliation. For contagion to occur, three conditions must be present: (1) a spatial concentration of assaultive violence, (2) a reciprocal nature to assaultive violence, and (3) escalations in assaultive violence. The reciprocal nature of gang violence accounts, in part, for how gangs form initially, as well as how they increase in size and strength of membership. The need to engage in retaliatory violence also helps explain the need for increasingly sophisticated weapons on the part of gang members. The knowledge that youths in a nearby neighborhood are united and may attack creates the need for an association to promote mutual protection. A gang fulfills this need. The threat of attack by a group of organized youths from another neighborhood is part of the gang belief system and helps to create the need for protection as well as to generate unity among a previously unorganized group of neighborhood youths. The concern that a rival gang is considering an attack often compels a peremptory strike (particularly drive-by shootings) from the gang that considers itself under threat. Rapid escalation of violence serves to explain the sudden peaks in gang violence. Attacks by one gang on another quickly lead to retaliatory strikes. These "spikes" observed in data on gang violence in Chicago (Block and Block, 1993) are conceptualized by Decker in the process shown in Figure 2-2.

Perhaps best known of community-level theories is "social disorganization," which dates back to Thrasher (1927). The tradition is traced to its contemporary context by Bursik and Grasmick (1993) and provides a foundation for Spergel's (1995) community mobilization approach to gang crime problems. Another community-level approach to gang crime and delinquency emphasizes the importance of culture. This perspective has been used effectively by Vigil (1988), Chin (1990), Moore (1991), and Padilla (1992). Hagedorn (1988) has stressed the importance of macroeconomic forces in explaining the development of the contemporary gang crime problem among urban African American populations. Dynamics in gang crime patterns across communities (Curry and Spergel, 1988) and across cities (Spergel and Curry, 1993) underscore the necessity to include community-level factors in our understanding of the link between gang membership and delinquency.

Multiple-Level Explanations

Spergel (1995, p. 146) proposed a model of gang involvement and gang-related crime and delinquency that includes all three levels of explanation. Decker and Van Winkle (1994, 1996; Decker 1996), in analyzing the gang crime problem in St. Louis, proposed a model that incorporates variations in perspective at the individual level, group process variables at the gang level, and community-level influences. This model is shown in Figure 2-3. Testing such multiple-level models will require systematic research designs that link longitudinal surveys to official records measures for individual and community areas, perhaps even in multiple cities. It is crucial, however, that these kinds of designs remain sensitive to what we have learned and are still learning from field studies.

Summary

It is important to keep in mind what we have already learned in almost a century of research about the impact of gang membership on participation in crime and delinquency. A list of key findings would have to include the following:

- Gang members are responsible for more crime and delinquency than their nongang counterparts.

- Gang crime and delinquency are predominantly violent in nature.

- There is considerable variation over time and communities in gangs and gang-related crime.

- Levels of gang crime and delinquency are more likely to be explained at the gang and community levels of explanation than at the individual level.

Chapter Three

The Gang Experience

Joe L. is an 18-year-old member of the Gangster Disciples in East St. Louis. Ironically, he is a white member of an almost all African American gang. Joe L. joined the Gangster Disciples at age 15, and has been extensively involved in criminal gang activities. He sells drugs and has participated in a number of drive-by shootings. He claims to have been arrested more than 50 times. In another irony, his parents both work, live in a middle-class neighborhood, and have sought counseling for him. He rejects his parent's overtures because of the allure of life in the gang. He doesn't expect to live much longer.

In this chapter, we document the gang experience largely from the perspective of gang members themselves. We draw from the results of a wide range of interviews, observations, and insights throughout the chapter. The critical point to be emphasized in this chapter is that the gang experience is a *dynamic process*, one that changes over time and across individuals. Here, we review such issues as joining gangs, initiation, getting "rank" in gangs, and leaving gangs. In addition we examine the *correlates* of gang involvement, such as age, race, and socioeconomic status of gang members. The chapter concludes with a discussion of the *organizational characteristics* of gangs, including the presence of leaders, rules, roles, and meetings. There is no single path that gang members follow, rather their experience is mediated by a variety of factors, including the correlates we examine in this chapter.

The Process of Gang Involvement

Joining a Gang

No single path exists that can capture the reasons or the processes by which individuals come to join a gang. But a key issue to understand in this context is whether individuals are *pulled* or *pushed* into gang membership. Young people who are pulled into membership join their gang because of the attractions it offers to them—the promise or expectation of friendship, opportunities to make money, or the ability to provide something for the neighborhood. Being pushed into the gang conveys a very different motivation for joining the gang. Individuals who see themselves as pushed into gang membership join their gang out of fear for physical consequences if they do not do so, or because they see themselves as powerless to resist the temptations of gang life.

There is considerable evidence to bear on this distinction, a distinction that is important because it can help to orient the nature of responses to the gang problem. Most available evidence supports the view that individuals are pulled toward their gangs because of what they see as the positive features of gang involvement. Most gang members report that they joined their gangs to be affiliated with their friends or because a number of their friends were members. Let's face it, teenagers have a powerful urge to be around their friends, and adolescence is a time of life when the need to affiliate with one's peers and reject or minimize the importance of relationships with parents is great. So this should come as no great surprise.

But hanging out with friends is not the only motivation for joining a gang. Indeed, a number of commentators (Skolnick, 1990; Sanchez-Jankowski, 1990; Padilla, 1992) report that the gang is a magnet for prospective members because of the promise of making money, typically through drug sales, but often through other crimes as well, such as robbery or burglary. (We shall further discuss drug sales in chapter 4.) Gang members routinely describe the opportunity to make money that membership in a gang offers them. And that opportunity is not one that requires long hours, hard work, and slow progression through the ranks. Selling drugs, whether by gang members or others, produces quick profits and is consistent with the desire for quick gratification that characterizes many adolescents' view of the relationship between work and money. Money provides other secondary attractions to gang membership, particularly as money allows its members to satisfy consumer needs (spending money on food, movies, CD's), and impress members of the opposite sex.

There are other attractive features to gang membership that pull young people toward a gang, particularly for many ethnic groups. In many communities, especially Latino/a, gangs represent a source of cultural pride and identification. Moore (1988), Vigil (1990), and Padilla (1992) all document the important role these gangs play in their communities by providing support for the neighborhood and broader cultural values. But we are only telling part of the story when we describe those who joined their gangs because of the attractive features of gang membership.

There is a darker side to the features of gangs and urban life that compel some young people to join their gang. A substantial fraction of young people join their gang seeking protection, either from rival gangs or just from the violence that lurks in many urban neighborhoods. Felix Padilla (1992) and Scott Decker and Barrik Van Winkle (1994, 1996; Decker, 1996) report that living in neighborhoods or attending schools with active gang members often produces the expectation that most young men are affiliated with a gang. Many young men reported to them that they eventually joined a gang because they got tired of being accused of being a member of one gang or another. Certainly living in a neighborhood dominated by one gang would lead outsiders to presume gang membership over time. But there is another reason, one more troubling, that compels many young people to join their gang—fear of the consequences of not being a member. Quite simply, a number of individuals are targeted for membership, either because of where they live, who they are, or the perception that they can be coerced into gang membership. This is especially likely in those neighborhoods where gangs dominate the local scene.

It is instructive to see once again the views of gang members. Reflecting their higher levels of organization, members of the Gangster Disciples who were being held in Joliet Prison in Illinois stated their views that the gang provided respect and instrumental values:

> Like if you give respect, you will be respected and not just because you are a part of the organization, because you respect an individual he gonna respect it. If you conduct yourself in a manner, in a

way that you want to be treated right then I will treat you the way you want to be treated.

Respect is an important issue in gang membership.

Other GD's in prison were less positive about the nature of gang membership:

The gang was a neighborhood thing, young, ignorant. It's not like people joined gangs for specific purposes, it's not like that.

But among established gangs in chronic gang cities like Chicago, there is a different character than in cities where gangs are just emerging:

I got cut across the face by opposition, Vice Lords, and although my family kept me away from that life, believe me, when this happened, they assessed the surrounding circumstances and automatically got in it.

I didn't even know at the time that I was in a gang. I was recognized because of my big brother and father were members.

And other imprisoned GDs saw joining the gang as part of the normal turn of events in their neighborhoods.

I wouldn't say I joined it, I wasn't forced, I joined it because it was the right thing to do at that appropriate time. I didn't see that by joining them it would be prosperous in any form or fashion, it was just something to do at the time, back then.

Another inmate offered a similar opinion:

Mainly growing up, my friends was into it [the Gangster Disciples] and I was around it so I fell into it.

San Diego gang members echoed the same reasons offered by Chicago gang members for joining their gang. Despite the differences in cities, the reasons were very similar. One offered that they joined out of "curiosity." For others, the neighborhood had a lot to do with getting in the gang.

I didn't really join. It was just where I stay, where I grew up at, that's where it was. Like you walk to the store or something or walk to school and they were all from the gang.

I think really I just wanted to get in it.

Actually what it is, it's just that you grow up with people and you hang together and you kind of watch each other's back. Someone come to your neighborhood and as long as it's one on one you let it go but if they bring another then you check 'em.

Gang members from St. Louis provided similar responses to questions about why they joined their gang. Most offered explanations that focused on informal explanations, or long-standing friendships:

I ain't going to say it's going to be my life but it was just something that came up to me where I was staying. I was just with the fellas and it just happened that I became one of them.

When I moved over here [to St. Louis] I started hanging with them. We herded together and stuff. I just started hanging with them.

To be in a gang you have friends. It's kinda good to be with some friends instead of going out cause if you ain't got no friends, it's really hard to get along out there.

Other gang members in St. Louis pointed to money as their motivation in joining the gang. However, even these gang members recognize the importance of the informal aspects of gang membership:

Money. Money and just being around a whole bunch of guys that like to do stuff that you like to do.

Help me make money. Help me protect myself. Really everything.

Initiation

Regardless of the motivation for joining a gang, becoming a member typically takes place over time, and the individual takes on a gang identity in a gradual process. But once the decision has been made (or as we noted for some cases, coerced) the next important step in the gang process is initiation. Nearly every documented gang in the United States has an initiation process, and there is variation in how initiation rituals occur. Most are rather crude with few formal aspects to them and involve some form of violence, typically by current members of the gang directed against the initiate.

The most common form of initiation reported is that of being "beaten in." Observers of the gang scene in Los Angeles, San Diego, St. Louis, Chicago, and Milwaukee (among other cities) report that this is the preferred method in most gang initiations. In this scenario, the individual being initiated either stands in the middle of a circle and must fight his or her way out, or must run between two lines of gang members (also known as the "gauntlet") who pummel him or her with their fists, feet, and occasionally other objects like bricks, rocks, and sticks. These initiations are often quite brutal, but end with "hugs" for the new member and the offering of a few words of unity for the gang. The fact that violence is a part of the very first experience within the gang is quite important. It sends a message to the new gang member that violence is important to the gang, is expected of all members, and constantly lurks beneath the surface of gang life.

This is not the only way that youth come to join their gangs. Often an older recruit or the sibling of a current gang member will be required to go on a "mission" against a rival gang. While this can take a variety of forms, it typically requires the recruit to fight or shoot a rival gang member, or conduct a crime such as robbery in rival gang territory. The initiation of female gang members merits comment at this time, though we deal with the issue of female gang membership in Chapter 5. Most observers of the girl gang scene report that girls tend to be initiated in the same way that boys are, through beating in, often by both boys and girls. A number of highly-publicized reports also document rapes of prospective female gang members. However, there is no widespread support for this as the typical way that girls are initiated into their gangs. Rather, the pattern that occurs for boys and girls appears to be similar.

The picture of life in a gang that has emerged to this point has emphasized the diversity of such experiences. The views of gang members are important in this regard. Again we present the views of active gang members on the issue of initiation. First, we examine the views of members of the Gangster Disciples from Chicago. They may be the most organized gang in the United States, yet they report initiation rituals similar to, if not less organized than, those in other cities.

> For the initiation, I had to prove my loyalty, prove how much I wanted to become a part of it and basically what I believed in.

To become a part of it, you just have to become sincere.

Other GDs said that they had to endure physical violence as part of their initiation:

Just get beat up.

And some members reported that they had to engage in crime:

Steal and hold drugs.

I proved myself through doing crimes.

Back then you had to prove your loyalty. So there was a guy that had turned State [evidence] on a member in the neighborhood and we took care of him.

The story was much the same in San Diego and St. Louis. Ironically, in these emerging gang cities, the initiation focused much more on violence. In almost all cases, potential gang members were "beaten in" as their initiation. In many cases, this was described as being "jumped in." The first four responses were from Chicano gang members in San Diego:

Some people get their ass kicked into the dirt.

Fist fighting. It was me against like three of them.

I had to prove to them that I'm down. Prove to them, get in fights.

Actually, they beat the crap out of me.

Their initiation experiences mirrored those of St. Louis gang members from African American gangs:

I had to have 15 dudes jump me.

Kill a couple of people, shoot them. Lay somebody on the ground and stomp them.

A whole bunch of dudes hit you.

I had to get into a fight, I had to lie there and be hit, take the pain.

Roles in a Gang

Later in this chapter we deal with the organizational structure of gangs. Here, however, we document the process by which individuals move from one status in a gang to a higher status. In Chapter 1 we distinguished between core and fringe members. Here we attempt to account for the steps members go through to move from one level in a gang to the next.

Most gangs are not very well organized, a point we will emphasize in greater detail later in this chapter. However, there are distinctions within gangs between the status and functions of some members. Indeed, in a few gangs in chronic gang cities like Chicago, these distinctions can be quite numerous and consequential. The process of acquiring rank is based primarily on length of time in the gang, blood relationships with current leaders, and level of criminal activity. Older gang members who have logged a considerable number of years as a member of their gangs (perhaps as many as five or six years as a member) are in a position to obtain rank and as a consequence are afforded special status and perform unique duties. Often referred to as OGs or original gangsters, these individuals hold the distinction of having lived through a number of years of gang life. But younger members who have a sibling who is a leader or otherwise influential in the gang may also be accorded rank. Finally, those whose criminal exploits, typically either involvement in violence or drug sales, are particularly noteworthy may also be accorded such status.

Rank brings certain obligations and expectations with it. Certain ceremonial functions of the gang, such as the initiation ritual or enforcing certain rules about colors, clothing styles, or behavior may be carried out by those with higher rank. And whatever gang planning that takes place is often conducted by these individuals. But there is also a symbolic function to rank, and that is to reinforce to younger or newer members the significance of the history of the gang and of gang members who may have died, gone to prison, or become separated from the gang for some reason.

It is instructive to examine what gang members say about the different roles in their gang. As noted above, gangs in emerging gang cities tend to have fewer roles, and those roles are not very well defined. Such gangs, in cities like Milwaukee, San Diego, San Antonio, Miami, Kansas City, and hundreds of other American cities (Curry, Ball and Decker, 1996) confirm this observation. For example, hear what a gang member in St. Louis said:

If we [the gang members] want something, all of us have to agree.

> Somebody say, let's go do this. Like one person say, I'll go. It be like half the people go this way and then if you don't want to go with them half will go that way and half will go this way.

These views were echoed by many San Diego gang members. Most of the San Diego gang members whose views we are familiar with reflected loosely organized gangs with few roles and little stability to those roles:

> There ain't no shot callers. It's got nothing to do with a gang either.

> They [all gang members] are equal, they are all hard core, they are all treated equal.

In those rare instances when different roles were identified, they would hardly qualify as highly specialized jobs that require differentiated skills:

> Yeah, there is different levels. There's some that just kick back and drink beer.

> It's not like, it's not levels. I respect my homeboy and he respects me, but I don't respect him more than I respect others.

> It's all one thing. It's just the older guys and then the youngsters.

However, our interviews with Gangster Disciples from Chicago, perhaps the best organized gang in the country, revealed quite a different picture. GDs could identify different roles by name and job and knew what it took to move from one role to another. These observations suggest a much more organized gang than found in most emerging gang cities:

> It goes from King, to the Board of Directors, the Generals, the First Captains. The rest is just the membership, the enforcers. Chairman, Board Members, Governors, Regents, Chief of Security, Foot soldiers.

The Latin Kings, a Latino/a gang in Chicago also had roles that were similar to those of the GDs:

> You got the Jefe, that's the highest. Then the Cacina, second. Soldiers, the lowest. There is the PeeWees and the Crowns.

Participating in Gang Violence

Violence is an important part of the gang experience. It is the motivation for many young people to join their gangs, is typically part of the initiation, and is ever present in the lives of most gang members. Understanding the role of violence in gangs is a key to learning more about the gang experience.

There is considerable evidence to show that gang members are both the victims and perpetrators of violence. The picture of gang members as victims of violence is quite sobering. In Chicago, the number of gang-motivated homicides increased fivefold between 1987 and 1992, and in Los Angeles County the number doubled in the same period. Most large cities with gang problems reported that in the early 1990s a larger and larger proportion of their cities' homicide victims were gang members. Some cities like Chicago and St. Louis reported that about one in four homicide victims were gang members; Los Angeles County reported that nearly half of its homicide deaths were gang members. Recall the study of St. Louis gang members by Decker and Van Winkle (1994, 1996; Decker, 1996). Of the 99 gang member subjects who participated in their study, 16 are now dead. This is a death rate that rivals that of soldiers in many recent wars.

Gang members commit homicides as well. Their participation as offenders parallels that as victims, which is to say that the 1990s have seen large surges in homicides—and other forms of violence—committed by gang members. The homicides committed by gang members have several distinctive characteristics that set them apart from other victims. First, gang violence is more likely than other crimes of violence to involve firearms, particularly handguns. The victims of gang homicide resemble their killers; that is, the victims of gang homicide are more likely to be the same in race, age, sex, and neighborhood where they live as the people who kill them. Surprisingly, most gang homicides lack a relationship to drug trafficking. Instead, gang homicides seem to be motivated by revenge or battles over turf.

But what accounts for all of this gang violence? These battles are rendered more lethal by the presence of guns—lots of guns. A number of observers have noted that the rise in crack cocaine trafficking in the mid-1980s produced the need for protection, usually in the form of guns. As the demand for guns increased, they became more plentiful, thus creating the need for more guns for "self-protection." The presence of more guns in the community has an escalating effect, increasing the likelihood that other young people would seek to own a gun. Support for this position comes in part from a study of over 8,000 arrestees who were interviewed shortly after their arrest. Gang members reported that they were more likely to own a gun, carry a gun most or all of the time, and have been victims of gun violence. Some have called this process a "contagion," spreading through communities much like a disease.

But violence has other less visible yet important consequences. Violence helps to hold gangs together. Most students of gangs have observed that the sources of gang solidarity are external to the gang and don't come from inside the gang. What this means in practice is that the threats posed by rival gangs, and sometimes police and other adult officials, help to create ties among gang members. It isn't hard to imagine that a pending attack from a gang in another neighborhood would create the need for cooperation and dependence among gang members. Often, after a violent act—real or imagined—gang members meet to discuss their role, discussions that help to create a legend for the gang, further soldifying the bonds between members.

Leaving a Gang

The first part of this chapter emphasized a number of the processes of gang life. We conclude this section by discussing the process of leaving a gang. There is considerable mythology about this aspect of gang life. Media reports have argued that it is impossible to leave a gang, or that in order to do so, a particularly heinous crime must be committed. We have even heard that gang members are told that they must kill one of their parents if they ever want to leave their gangs. Fortunately, there is evidence that can be reviewed on this issue, and (even more fortunately) it dispels these myths.

Studies of gangs from a number of cities—Chicago, Los Angeles, Milwaukee, San Diego, St. Louis—report a large number of ex-gang members. Interviews with former members document that most of them simply quit their gangs in the same way they ended other affiliations. Decker and Lauritsen (1996) interviewed two dozen former gang members in St. Louis, and found that most quit their gangs simply by announcing their intentions to do so and leaving. In reality, acting out that decision was somewhat more difficult, since the gangs represented the source of many friends as well as important relationships and activities. Few of those who left their gangs reported that they faced physical consequences for doing so, though a few former members said that they were threatened with violence but that the threats were never carried out. Interestingly, most of those who left their gangs continued to associate with members of their old gangs.

Motivations for leaving a gang are also important to understand. The St. Louis sample of ex-members cited their concerns about escalating violence as one of the reasons they decided to end their affiliation with their gangs and move on with their life. Key in this process was the witnessing of a violent act committed against a fellow gang member or being a victim themselves. Others reported that the obligations of life, such as a job, becoming a parent, or getting older, were the key reasons that motivated them to end their relationship with the gang.

Correlates of Gang Involvement

Who joins gangs, and what does the typical gang member look like? These are the questions we explore in this section of the book. But we caution you, even as we try to answer these questions, that there are no simple answers and the answers are changing because gangs are dynamic social institutions in American society. Perilous a task as it is, in this section we examine the correlates of gang membership—age, race, and socioeconomic status.

A number of studies have examined these correlates, and most that do include the issue of age. Gang members range across a wide variety of ages, but typically they are teenagers. It is not easy to pinpoint a single age as the "average" age of gang members, but a number of studies identify 17 or 18 as the average age of members in their sample. These figures come from police estimates, independent researchers, and government figures, so we can have confidence in them because they are the product of multiple sources. Gang members can be quite young, however, as some researchers have documented gang members as young as 12 years of age. It is difficult to document core members much younger than 12 because of the difficulty assigning credibility to claims of membership by individuals much younger than that age, though we are confident that such do exist. There are also gang members who are (relatively speaking) quite old, certainly in their 40s. As the gang phenomenon in the United States "matures," and spans a larger number of years, it is reasonable to expect that the number of older gang members will grow. And that fact produces problems for communities that are attempting to intervene and do something about their gang problems.

One of the more contentious issues in addressing gangs is determining the race and ethnic status of gang members. There is considerable concern that racial and ethnic minorities are over identified as gang members, largely as a consequence of the ability and intention of people in positions of power and influence to make the acts of minority members criminal. Some (Brown, 1977) have gone so far as to claim that gangs represent an extension of the African American family, while others state that identifying young African American males as gang members is part of an effort to subjugate an entire race. The exclusion of skinheads and hate groups from the definition of gangs adds to the concern over the use of gang terms to describe the behavior of minority group members.

In the midst of this debate, we would like to offer our perspective on the racial and ethnic composition of gangs. The national surveys of police departments reviewed in Chapter 1 provide strong evidence that racial and ethnic minorities, particularly African Americans and Latinos/as, are the primary members of gangs. Indeed, these surveys show that, according to police estimates, 48 percent of gang members are African Americans, and 43 percent are Latinos/as. The balance are 5 percent Asian American and 4 percent white (Curry, Ball, and Fox 1994a). Police data, however, are subject to the charge that they are biased and overrepresent the participation of minorities. However, police data are substantially corroborated by the results of field studies and surveys. Though field studies purposely target a specific gang or neighborhood, collectively they generally support the view derived from surveys of police that African Americans and Latinos/as dominate gang membership.

The results from surveys provide a picture consistent with that from police and field studies. Esbensen and Huizinga (1993) and Thornberry et al. (1993) conducted extensive surveys of youths regarding gang membership. The Esbensen study was conducted in Denver, and Thornberry's work was completed in Rochester, New

York. Esbensen found that whites comprised a larger percentage of gang members than was the case for the police surveys. Thornberry reported findings consistent with the work from Denver. These results suggest that racial minorities, especially African Americans and Latinos/as, comprise the majority of gang members in the United States. This is hardly surprising, given our earlier review of the history of gangs in this country. As we noted earlier, gangs tend to attract individuals who find themselves at the bottom of the social and economic ladder in society. Just as the gangs of the 1890s and 1920s were largely comprised of Irish and Italian youth, representing groups struggling for inclusion in the economic and social mainstream, Latinos/as and African Americans comprise the modal category of gang membership.

There is evidence that gangs are becoming more interracial. As we noted earlier, gangs tend to draw their members from their neighborhoods. To the extent that neighborhoods are comprised of diverse residents, gangs will represent that diversity. Decker and Van Winkle (1994, 1996; Decker, 1996) in St. Louis found that most African American gangs were willing to include white members, and that whites played important roles in those gangs.

The next correlate of gang membership we consider is the socioeconomic status of members. It is not surprising that the majority of gang members come from the lowest socioeconomic groups in American society. This was the case for the three earlier gang cycles in our country's history. A number of commentators (Jackson,1991; Hagedorn, 1988; Decker and Van Winkle, 1994, 1996; Decker, 1996) have observed that gangs are located in cities and neighborhoods with large concentrations of urban poor. This observation seems a logical consequence of the historical characteristics of gangs, but there is evidence that gang membership is more complicated than socioeconomic status alone. The emergence of gangs in suburbs and rural areas presents a challenge to the view that gang members are drawn exclusively from the poorest members of society. Clearly, the concentrations of poverty and isolation that characterize the experiences of many minority group members in large American cities provide fertile recruiting grounds for gangs. However, poverty is not destiny, as most poor youth do not join gangs, and a growing number of middle- and upper-class youths are becoming gang members.

Characteristics of Gang Organization

How organized are gangs? Do gangs have the organizational features of organized crime groups or legitimate businesses? These are the questions that frame the third and final section of this chapter. Here we examine questions such as whether gangs have leaders, rules, roles, meetings, punishments for violating rules, and the extent to which they coordinate revenue-generating activities and the investment of money generated from such activities.

One view of gang organization is that of the vertically organized gang, a gang that has a formal structure that enforces rules and acts in the same ways that a business may act. An alternative view argues that most gangs are horizontal and lack the formal-rational character of organizations with established leadership structures and well-defined roles and missions. As is generally the case with gangs, there is considerable diversity regarding the answer to these questions. However, in general it is our view that gangs do not tend to be very well organized.

Gang Leaders

Most gangs have leaders. This should not be very surprising, as few organizations can survive without some form of leadership. However, gang leaders in most cases are less likely to resemble corporate executives as they are to be like captains of sports teams, a role that can change from one circumstance or one day to another. Not surprisingly, leadership roles are better defined in those gangs and gang cities where gangs have operated the longest. Thus, in Chicago and Los Angeles, we find gang leaders who are older, more specialized in their activities, and more powerful. In other cities, those we have called emerging gang cities, leadership roles have a far more informal character. In these gangs, the leader of a gang can change from one day or one function to another. Typically, among these less-organized gangs, leaders are chosen from among the ranks of those who have been members the longest, are the toughest, or are the most involved in crime. As gang membership entails much criminal activity, it is not surprising to find that leaders change regularly, as members go to prison. In the most organized Chicago gangs like the Gangster Disciples, going to prison often enhances the status of an individual in the gang, and many leadership activities take place from the state or federal prison system.

The following quotes from gang members describe the diversity of leadership that exists in most gangs. Not unexpectedly, gang members from Chicago report well-defined leadership roles and leadership qualities:

> Leaders give orders.

> The king, he is the overseer. He's the guy that, OK, if the generals come together and want to lay down a productive program they will first converse with the king. See how the king like the program. If the king don't like the program, if they suggest a program and the king doesn't like it, if he says don't do it, they won't touch it, they won't touch it at all.

> Leaders take on full responsibility as to guiding an organization, keeping within the guidelines of the organization that Larry Hoover [the imprisoned leader of the Gangster Disciples in Chicago] set out for us to abide by.

> The leader makes the rules and everybody got to do what he say.

The picture of leadership found in San Diego and St. Louis gangs was quite different from that in Chicago. Indeed, most of the gang members we talked with in St. Louis and San Diego couldn't identify leadership roles.

In addition, most of the gangs in those cities reported that they changed leaders on a routine basis:

> Everybody calls their own shots. Nobody has the juice.

> We all together. We had a leader but since he's a dead homie, we ain't got another one.

Others in St. Louis identified the leader as someone who was the oldest member of the gang, or the biggest.

Gang Rules

In order to survive, most organizations need rules. Gangs are no different in this respect. When asked, every gang member we know of would say that his or her gang had rules and could list several. However, the character of those rules helps us to understand the nature of gang organization. A relatively small number of gangs have actual written sets of rules, constitutions; by far most gangs simply have a set of rules that are understood among the members. Most important among these are prohibitions against snitching on other gang members to the police, cheating other gang members from their deserved profits from illegal activity, and pretending to be a member of another gang by wearing the "wrong" colors or giving the wrong hand signs. However, these rules hardly resemble the criminal code or a set of formal rules adopted by a corporation. The exceptions again come from Los Angeles and Chicago, our two most chronic gang cities. A number of gangs in these cities have written constitutions.

One of the ways that we attempt to understand the importance of rules for any organization is whether there are formal punishments or mechanisms to mete out punishment for those who violate the rules. Punishments that are informal, "made up" on the spur of the moment, have less force and reflect the character of a less-organized group than those punishments that are specified in the rules themselves. For example, the criminal code of your state specifies both the behavior that is illegal, like stealing a car or breaking into someone's residence, as well as the punishment for that behavior, such as two to ten years in the state penitentiary. These formal rules are examples from highly developed organizations. In addition, the mechanism by which punishment can be meted out is specified in the rules. In the case of the criminal code, the due process rights, jury selection procedures, and other procedural rules are all found in the written code.

No gang we know of has a system of rules, punishments, and judicial procedures quite so formal. Indeed, most gangs have what we regard as informal systems of punishments. The punishment an individual receives can depend on who he or she is and who is deciding on the punishment as much as what the gang member did. This should hardly be surprising. After all, as we noted earlier in this chapter, the average age of gang members is 17 or 18. We would not expect to find elaborate, formal systems of rules, punishments, and procedures developed by young people, whose lives generally are not characterized by the desire for order and regularity that is the case for adults. Where penalties do exist, they are likely to include elements of physical violence, being beaten in the circle such as is the case for initiations, or being exiled from the gang.

When a group has rules, with a method for determining infractions and penalties, it is more organized than if there were no rules. Thus, we regard the presence of rules, a system to determine violations, and punishments to be important features in distinguishing the level of gang organization. In general, the more organized a gang is, the better defined its rules will be. Most gangs do not have well-defined rules.

Gangs in emerging cities are far less likely to have a well-defined system of rules and punishments. In spite of this general tendency, some minimal rules do exist, or it would not be possible for the organization to exist. In some cases, rules function in symbolic ways; in other cases the enforcement of rules helps to keep the gang functioning. A St. Louis gang member reported that the rules were, "Don't steal from me. Don't snake your partner out. And uh, don't lie." Others told us that there weren't really rules. "Ain't no rules, just do what comes to mind."

San Diego gang members echoed these sentiments. One member offered that the only rule was, "Not to backstab your partner. That's the main one." Another reported, "Don't ever snitch on your own homeboys." Similarly, we were told that the main rule for the gang was, "Not to get out of line."

When we interviewed Chicago gang members, however, we heard quite a different story. Rules among Chicago gang members were more formal, had penalties attached, and under some circumstances had a formal procedure for determining when a rule violation occurred. Most of the rules focused on concealing the nature of the gang from outsiders. One final characteristic was found in these rules—they were written. Some of the rules were focused on what the gang should invest its money in, clear evidence of direction in the gang. A number of gang members from the Gangster Disciples and Latin Kings talked of gang constitutions. These constitutions are treated by members as confidential documents.

> They got two sets of law, 1 through 16, and 1 through 22. Each and every member has to study and learn the laws because the only way you can be in violation based on the gang's philosophy is to violate one of those laws.

> They are written down until you learn them. You got a certain amount of time to learn them.

> The most important rule, once a king, always a king and they don't have no rapists. No rapists, no heroin users.

Gang Roles

Up to this point, we have defined gangs as being either formal or informal organizations. There are substantial differences between these two types. There is one organizational issue, however, on which the two types of gangs converge: the presence of specialized roles within the gang. Almost all gangs distinguish between the roles members play in the gang. In the least-organized case, this distinction is only between core and fringe members, with the former participating more fully in decisions about activities. But few gangs are quite so informal in their identification of roles. In most gangs there are at least three role levels: (1) leaders, (2) experienced gang members, and (3) regular members, the majority of members. Leadership roles are occupied by the smallest number of gang members. These roles typically include individuals who have been in the gang the longest or have achieved some distinctive status as a consequence of their criminal activity or bravado. More experienced gang members may assume some specialized role within the gang, such as converting powder cocaine to crack, obtaining weapons, or stealing cars. These individuals are likely to have been members of the gang for at least two to three years and have earned their rank as a consequence of special skills or achievements. The majority of members play few specialized roles and offer little to the gang beyond simply being regular members.

Roles are not just the property of individuals but also exist for specific activities. It is often the case that a number of distinct roles are necessary to successfully sell drugs, particularly crack cocaine. Some may be more adept at making the connections to get large amounts of the product, while others "rock it up," and others serve as lookouts, contacts, or actually sell the product. These roles are often interchangeable, and yesterday's lookout can be today's seller.

Gang Meetings and Money

Another aspect of gang organization is whether or not the gang holds regular meetings. The available evidence indicates that, in some form or another, most gangs do hold meetings. However, these meetings rarely look like the meetings of a large corporation or government agency. Indeed, they rarely even resemble a faculty meeting or the meeting of a local men's or women's organization. The informal character that typifies most gangs also can be found in the nature of their meetings. It is not easy to speak of the average size of gangs in this country, as there is considerable variation. However, in most cities gangs average between 50 and 250 members. It is difficult to imagine all 250 members of the Rolling Sixties Crips in St. Louis or the Calle Triente in San Diego gathering in a park or at a mall to have a meeting. Meetings, when they do occur, are much more likely to involve a small group of key decision makers who then funnel the word on to other members.

The final aspect of gang structure and organization is what happens to the money that the gang's activities generate. Indeed, one of the keys to understanding any organization is to understand what happens to money generated by members of the organization. In some cases, all of the money is reinvested in the organization so that it can grow. In other cases, the money raised by members of an organization is kept by the individuals for their own use. The first model is the corporate model, and the second is a model of individual entrepreneurship. With few exceptions, gangs function as entrepreneurial organizations, where individuals sell drugs or commit crimes for their own benefit, rarely, if ever, reinvesting their profits into the larger gang. We did note that there were a few exceptions, and if you have been reading this book at all closely, you would guess that Chicago would be a location where we could find a model that looks more like the corporate model. Certainly among the Gangster Disciples and the Black Gangster Disciples, reinvestment in the gang is an important priority, and profits from drug sales are often used to buy legal businesses, in much the same way as organized crime leverages illegal money into the legal market. It is possible that certain Chicago gangs are becoming organized crime groups as financial activities are taking on a more organized character. Indeed, the Internal Revenue Service and the U.S. Attorney's Office have recently successfully prosecuted gang members in Chicago, ironically in much the same way that Al Capone was eventually prosecuted and convicted.

Summary

We have reviewed many important aspects of the gang experience, including gang processes, correlates of gang involvement, and characteristics of gang organization. It is important to keep in mind one of the central premises of this book: a key to understanding gangs is understanding who their members are and what they are like. The majority of members are in their teens, a time of life that is not characterized by high levels of formal or organized behavior. We ought not be surprised then, that by and large gangs lack the characteristics of formal organizations and that the processes of membership reflect the sometimes haphazard nature of adolescence.

Chapter Four

Gangs, Gang Members, and Drug Sales

In this chapter we examine the role of gangs and gang members in the sale and distribution of drugs. Here we pay particular attention to what current research and law enforcement knowledge show about the impact of gangs on drug distribution. We will examine the unique contribution that gangs and gang members make to drug sales, and how large a role drug sales play in the lives of gang members.

There are two competing views about the role of gangs and gang members in drug sales. The first argues that street gangs are well-organized purveyors of illegal drugs who reinvest the profits from drug sales into the gangs. The authors of this view see gangs involved in drugs sales in very substantial and direct ways. A second approach rejects this notion. Its proponents claim that drug sales by gangs are seldom well-organized and gang members often act independently of their gangs in selling drugs. This view sees the link between gangs and drug sales as much more casual. Two issues that are critical to understanding the link between gangs and drugs are the organizational aspects of gangs and the nature of the street drug market. We pay attention to both issues throughout this chapter.

Concern about the role of street gangs and their members in drug sales has grown in the last decade. Because street gangs and crack cocaine emerged at about the same time in many cities, a number of observers have drawn a causal link between the two. Such concerns reflect the view of federal and local law enforcement that such activities are well organized and have national connections (National Institute of Justice, 1993b). This view has received considerable support, especially from those within the criminal justice system.

In order to effectively control drug sales, gangs must possess several characteristics. First, gangs must have an organizational structure. This hierarchy must have leaders, roles, and rules. Second, gangs must have group goals that are widely shared among members. Third, gangs must promote stronger allegiance to the larger organization than to subgroups within it. Finally, gangs must possess the means to control and discipline their members to produce compliance with group goals. This view of gangs as formal-rational organizations is inconsistent with descriptions of gangs from studies from the 1970s (Klein, 1971; Short and Strodtbeck, 1974; Moore, 1978). James Short (1974), in commenting about the level of organization and status of goals within gangs, observed:

> Individual gangs, such as the Vice Lords and the Stones, sometimes have given the appearance of moving from largely expressive to more instrumental goals; but the extent to which such changes are in fact real is far from clear. (p. 426)

But have gangs changed in the last generation? Recent evidence has emerged to support the notion that—at least when it comes to drug sales—some gangs do operate as formal-rational organizations.

This chapter addresses a number of questions regarding gang involvement in drug sales. Specifically, we examine the extent of involvement, level of organization, and motives of gang members in selling drugs. We accomplish this by reviewing a large number and variety of sources of information about the activities of gang members.

Framing the Debate

There are essentially two positions in the debate about gang involvement in drug sales. They are best represented by Jerome Skolnick and his colleagues (1988; Skolnick, 1990), and Martin Sanchez-Jankowski (1991) on the one hand, and by Malcolm Klein, Cheryl Maxson, and Lea Cunningham (1991; Klein and Maxson, 1994), and Decker and Van Winkle (1994, 1996; Decker, 1996) on the other. The first group of researchers describe gangs as formal-rational organizations with a leadership structure, roles, rules, common goals, and control over members. The second group of researchers describes gangs as loosely confederated groups generally lacking in persistent forms of cohesion or organization. The extent and nature of gang involvement in drug sales is derived from these views of organizational structure.

Gangs as Formal-Rational Organizations

Based on interviews with 39 inmates in state correctional facilities and 42 police and correctional officials, Jerome Skolnick and his colleagues (1988; Skolnick, 1990) argued that many gangs are organized solely for the purpose of selling drugs. They found that the involvement of gangs in drug distribution is well organized and provided the primary motivation for membership, and that many gangs in California effectively controlled the drug markets in their territories. They distinguished between "entrepreneurial" gangs and what they called "cultural gangs," territorially based neighborhood gangs. Cultural gangs were not involved in street drug sales in a causal way. These gangs used violence to maintain their identity in the neighborhood, primarily against rival gangs, for expressive purposes.

The entrepreneurial gangs, found mostly in northern California and among African American gangs in Los Angeles, had a much stronger commitment to street drug sales. In fact, their reason for existing and the motivation for individuals to join the gang arose from their involvement in street drug sales. Skolnick et al. (1988) argued that many of these gangs are "organized solely for the purpose of distributing drugs" (p. 4). The gang offered many rational advantages for individuals interested in selling drugs, including protection, controlled territory in which to sell, rules that proscribe turning in a fellow gang member, and a wealth of market information. Members of these gangs perceived membership to be permanent and saw themselves as "organized criminals." These findings are consistent with the view of gangs as formal-rational organizations.

Martin Sanchez-Jankowski (1991) depicted gangs as well-organized groups with strongly held group goals. In a study based on 10 years of field work with 37 gangs representing six different ethnic groups in three cities, Sanchez-Jankowski described gangs as highly structured organizations. Despite being comprised of "defiant individualists" (p. 23), he described gangs as highly rational organizations with formal leadership structures, roles, codes of conduct, and specific duties. Consistent with this description of gangs, he argued that gangs have collective economic goals and that members contribute time and efforts toward the achievement of these goals. These efforts resulted in the creation of capital to pursue both legal and illegal activities. Drug sales played a primary role in such pursuits, and consequently were well organized and effectively managed. The collective use of the profits from drug sales for gang purposes, such as the purchase of businesses or expanding drug markets, are evidence of the effective management of drug sales.

Support for the formal-rational view is found in Carl Taylor's (1990; 1993) fieldwork with Detroit gangs. Taylor identified three types of gangs: (1) scavenger gangs, (2) territorial gangs, and (3) corporate gangs. The latter were well-organized gangs with effective leaders and widely shared group goals. They had evolved from less-organized structures to what Taylor identified as the "big leagues" (1993, p. 99) of drug distribution. Members of these gangs ran drug sales like a business, and Taylor compared them to Fortune 500 companies. For Taylor, the key to understanding the evolution of gangs from relatively disorganized neighborhood groups to their highly structured state was their level of organization. Effective drug distribution requires strong leadership, commitment to organizational goals, and powerful rewards. Taylor found that corporate gangs possessed all of these attributes.

Tom Mieczkowski (1986) studied the heroin distribution network of Young Boys Incorporated (YBI), an African American gang in Detroit. Using the results of a field study of 15 male gang members, Mieczkowski characterized heroin street sales as rational, being conducted by a highly organized gang. Street sales were coordinated by a leader who enforced a system of discipline based on rules generally accepted by all members of the gang. Individuals were specifically recruited to sell heroin, held specific roles in the distribution network, and operated within a "bureaucratic" structure. Similarly, Felix Padilla (1992) characterized drug sales by Puerto Rican gangs in Chicago as an "ethnic enterprise" (p. 3). Based on the results of a year-long ethnography, he found the viability of the gangs he studied depended on their ability to make money. He discovered specific criminal roles in the gang, the most prestigious of which was street dealing. However, large capital was not accumulated and gang members generally used the profits from drug sales to support individual commodity needs.

Gangs as Adaptive and Informal Groups

The image of gangs as well-organized groups sharing common goals in the sale of drugs stands in stark contrast to findings from Los Angeles, the area of the country with the most gangs. Malcolm Klein et al. (1991) and Ira Reiner (1992) both argued that gangs lack the organizational structure and commitment to common goals to be successful in drug sales. In an extensive report, Reiner (at the time, the District Attorney of Los Angeles County) observed that gangs in Los Angeles did not control drug sales because they were disorganized and had a loosely confederated structure. Reiner found that traditional street gangs were not well suited for drug distribution or any other business-like activity and that they were weakly organized, prone to unnecessary and unproductive violence, and full of brash, conspicuous, untrustworthy individuals who drew unwanted police attention. For all these reasons, Reiner argued, big drug operators—those who turned to drug dealing as a serious career—typically de-emphasized gang activity or left the gang altogether (1992, p. 97).

Klein et al. (1991) used police arrest records from five Los Angeles area police stations to examine the differences between crack sales involving gang members and those of nongang members. Klein and his colleagues were interested in several specific hypotheses, particularly that crack increased the control of drug markets by gangs and that increases in violence were linked to the disproportionate involvement of gang members in crack sales. They found no support for either of these contentions, underscoring that each was based on a conception of the nature of gang organizational structure and social processes at variance with the sociological literature on gangs. Central to their concerns were the lack of an effective organizational structure within gangs, absence of permanent membership or roles, and lack of shared goals. Compared to nongang transactions, gang crack sales were more likely to occur on the street, involve firearms, include younger suspects, and disproportionately involve African American suspects. However, most of these differences were small. In other words, the characteristics associated with crack sales by gang members weren't much different from those of nongang members. Klein et al. (1991) concluded by noting that gang membership added little of a distinctive nature to street drug sales and that, while the problems associated with gangs and drug sales intersected, they were not a single problem (p. 635).

One of the dilemmas in using data from inmates or police files is that the data have undergone a considerable filtering process. In an attempt to circumvent this concern, a number of researchers have interviewed gang members directly. Jeffrey Fagan (1989) interviewed 151 gang members through a snowball sampling procedure in 1984 and 1985 in high-crime neighborhoods in Los Angeles, Chicago, and San Diego. In general, gang members reported lower levels of drug sales than nongang members, especially compared with their levels of participation in other forms of crime. These findings provide support for the contention that selling drugs is not the primary motivation for joining a gang nor the primary outlet for gang activities. Based on the nature of activities they engaged in, Fagan offered four typologies of gangs. For two of the gang types, social gangs and serious delinquents, drug sales were not a primary activity. Taken together, these gangs included nearly two-thirds of the individuals interviewed. However, for party gangs and emerging organizations, drug sales were a major focus of activity. Despite their involvement in drug sales, party gangs lacked structure, rules, and roles, elements considered essential for the control of drug markets and not found among serious delinquents and emerging organizations. Fagan concluded by noting that, regardless of type, gang life was characterized by "informal social processes" and provided an opportunity to "hang out" more than a formal structure within which to make money.

Joe Sheley, Joseph Shang, and Jim Wright (1993) analyzed the results of a survey completed by 381 self-identified male gang member inmates in California, Illinois, Louisiana, and New Jersey and 835 males in six juveniles facilities in those states. Three types of gangs were identified based on their level of organization: (1) quasi gangs, (2) unstructured gangs, and (3) structured gangs. Consistent with the results of Fagan (1989) and Klein et al. (1991), they argued that informal group processes dominated gang activities, including involvement in drug sales. There were no differences in drug sales between gang types, or gang and nongang inmates.

John Hagedorn (1988) interviewed 47 gang members from 19 of Milwaukee's largest gangs. He characterized gangs as dynamic, evolving associations of adolescents and men. In general, gangs lacked formal roles and effective organizational structures for achieving consensus among members regarding goals or techniques for achieving those goals. Hustling (including street drug sales) was seldom well organized because gangs lacked the organizational structure to control their members effectively. Only about one-half of the members sold drugs, and the proceeds of such sales provided only modest income. Hagedorn (1994a) obtained similar results when he conducted additional interviews in 1993. The gang leaders he interviewed in the 1980s remained involved in the sale of drugs, but they continued to do so in a fashion consistent with their earlier involvement.

In a study of urban drug sales and the effect of the underground economy on licit work, Fagan (1992) examined the drug market in two distressed New York City neighborhoods. Using chain referral sampling techniques, he recruited 1,003 subjects from a variety of sources to create a sample broadly representative of drug arrestees. Most drug sales had a relatively disorganized character; that is, groups of individuals involved in street drug sales (primarily crack cocaine) had little structure and operated on an informal basis. Most associations were temporary and individuals tended to "float" in and out of drug sales. The money earned from drug sales was used for short-term concerns, given to family members, spent on items of food, clothing, or gifts for members of the opposite sex. Fagan concluded by noting that drug sales have become institutionalized, but few of his findings support the argument that drug selling has become a formal role for specific individuals.

Surveys of the general population as a means to understand gangs are rare. However, Esbensen and Huizinga (1993) used data from the Denver Youth Survey, a longitudinal study of families and youth, to understand the involvement of gang and nongang members in a number of illegal activities. Both male and female gang members were distinguished from nongang members by the increased prevalence and incidence of their criminal behaviors. That is, more gang members committed crimes and did so at a higher rate than nongang members. However, the level of drug sales between the two groups was about the same. These results suggested that more gang members sell drugs than their nongang counterparts, but that gang involvement in street drug sales does not increase the frequency of sales. Interestingly, Esbensen and Huizinga characterized gangs as informal organizations lacking structure. Furthermore members of their sample could not agree on a common gang definition. Finally, most gang members reported that membership in their gang was of relatively short duration, typically about a year.

William Sanders (1994) conducted a 10-year study of gangs in San Diego, primarily by making observations while riding with police patrols and interviewing individuals referred to him by the police. In general, he argued that social scientists depict gangs as "overstructured." In his view gang structure and control over members were far different than typically described. While the focus of his study was primarily on gang violence, his results made it clear that gangs fail to organize or control the profits from drug sales effectively.

Decker and Van Winkle (1994, 1996; Decker, 1996) conducted a three-year field study of gangs in St. Louis in the early 1990s. Almost all gang members in the study (95 percent) reported having sold drugs at some time in their life, making them similar to those interviewed by Fagan (1992). The primary drug sold by gang members was crack cocaine; little marijuana or heroin was sold. Despite the ready availability of crack, few gang members reported using the drug despite their regular use of marijuana. Few gang members reported that they joined their gang for the opportunity to sell drugs; instead, they affiliated with the gang for expressive reasons having to do with prior associations in the neighborhood. The majority of respondents (58 percent) could not identify specific roles played by members of the gang in drug sales. The category most often reported by those who did identify a role, however, was as "seller," hardly evidence of a highly structured or rational organization. A crucial aspect of any organized entrepreneurial activity is what happens to the profits. If street gangs organize and control drug sales, it is reasonable to assume that part of the profits of such sales would be re-invested into the gangs. Virtually all of the gang members reported that they used the profits from drug sales for individual consumption, such as to buy clothes, fast food or compact discs, not to meet gang objectives. Decker and Van Winkle supported the contention that drug sales by gang members lack formal roles and are not well organized.

Summary

Despite the diversity of methods employed, the second group of studies provides a rather consistent picture of the role of gangs and gang members in drug sales. These conclusions stand in stark contrast to the findings of Sanchez-Jankowski, Skolnick, Mieczkowski, Padilla, and Taylor, who argue that gangs bring a high level of organization to drug sales. Despite the evidence to the contrary, many public officials, especially those in law enforcement (NIJ, 1993) continue to express the belief that gang involvement in drug sales more closely resembles the model presented by Sanchez-Jankowski and Skolnick.

This chapter suggests three central questions to be answered in attempting to determine the nature of gang involvement in drug sales. These can be organized around three primary issues. First, we need to document how extensively gang members are involved in drug sales. Most of the evidence suggests that gang members have substantial involvement in the sale of drugs. Most gang members sell drugs, though the level at which they sell may not be increased by gang membership alone.

A second issue is to determine how gang members organize drug sales. An effective organizational structure would be necessary to sustain prolonged, successful drug sales and distribution of drug profits. Gangs with a vertical organization or hierarchy would be more likely to conduct effective drug sales than those with horizontal or temporary configurations. Evidence of such a structure could be observed in a variety of mechanisms, such as the distribution of profits or development of specific roles.

Finally, the existence of common goals within the gang is an important indicator of the level of gang organization in drug sales. Organizations with common goals strongly held by their members should be able to organize drug sales. Specifically, we need to know if the profits from drug sales are spent for group or individual purposes.

One of the most difficult issues in studying gangs is distinguishing between the activities of individual gang members and those of the gang as James Short did in his reasearch (1985). Short distinguished between large aggregates (like gangs), smaller aggregations of individuals (such as gang subgroups), and individuals. The conclusions of this chapter indicate that these are important distinctions, and that being a member of a gang is not a "master status" in the sense that it controls the behavior of an individual gang member. Rather, individual gang members often act on their own or in subgroups outside their gangs, a distinction that applies to the noncriminal and criminal activities of gang members, including drug sales. It is possible for an individual gang member to engage in drug sales outside the structure or influence of his or her gang or subgroup.

Skolnick et al. (1988, p. 3) and others suggest that the profits from drug sales act as a powerful magnet, attracting potential members to the gang and leading to well-coordinated drug sales. However, many studies suggest that the reasons for joining a gang are expressive, reflecting the group process of neighborhood networks and friendships. Because of this, the extent of involvement, level of organization, and use of profits from drug sales remain consistent with the view of Klein et al. (1991) and Fagan (1989) that gang involvement in street drug sales reflects their loose organizational structure. The common theme that unites these findings points to the group processes involved in gang membership and the strength of the ties that bind gang members to their gangs. In most cities in the 1990s, gangs appear to be loosely confederated associations of young men and women united through shared expressive concerns over protection of turf, reputation, and threats to the safety of themselves or other members of their gang. Commitments to instrumental concerns—money—are expressed only with regard to pursuits of more immediate gratification such as obtaining money for clothes or parties. This view of gang structure and activity is consistent with findings from a number of different cities, for different ethnic groups, and based on different research strategies (Moore, 1978; 1991; Klein, 1971; Klein and Maxson, 1994; Hagedorn, 1988; Miller, 1958; Sanders, 1994; Short and Strodtbeck, 1974, Vigil, 1988). Indeed, as others have suggested (Klein et al., 1991; Reiner, 1992), the gang is unsuited for the tasks of building consensus among its members and organizing their activities, characteristics essential for a successful business operation. To a great extent, this is because most gang members were focused on short-term needs, to the virtual exclusion of long-term concerns. These impediments—the lack of structure and goals—would also prevent gangs from effectively organizing other profit-making, ventures such as burglary, robbery, or auto theft.

The difference between Skolnick's findings and the research of Moore, Hagedorn, Sanders, Klein and his colleagues, and Decker and Van Winkle cannot be linked simply to differences in the method of study. Sanchez-Jankowski, Taylor, and Padilla used field-based methods and arrived at the conclusion that drug sales were well-organized. However, Moore, Hagedorn, Sanders, Decker, and Van Winkle also used field-based techniques to recruit and interview gang members and arrived at distinctively different conclusions about the role of gang members in drug sales. It is interesting to observe that Klein and his colleagues used police data and yet failed to establish a distinctive role for gang members in drug sales, specifically the selling of rock cocaine. Klein's research was conducted in Los Angeles, identified by Spergel and Curry (1994) as a chronic gang city. Similarly, Padilla found that ethnic gangs in Chicago, another chronic gang city, were modestly organized. However, his findings stand in contrast to those of Skolnick, who argued for a formal-rational character to gang drug sales that resembles the way corporate America goes about business.

One key to understanding street drug sales lies in understanding the market. The urban drug market is primarily a crack market; its customers are not involved in organized networks that characterize the distribution of other drugs. Crack users generally lead disorganized lives and their need for the drug is powerful, often resulting in "crack runs," periods of intense use. Their desire for the drug creates demand for a market that provides easy and open access for its customers. As MacCoun and Reuter (1992) have demonstrated, street-level drug dealing is a sporadic occupation, used to supplement other sources of income. Such markets are more likely to be served by the episodic and loosely organized gang members (among others) engaged in selling drugs than they are by well-organized, persistent groups.

Chapter Five

Female Gang Involvement

Yolanda is a 19-year-old member of the Hoover Crips. Her gang is related to a male-dominated set of Hoover Crips. She joined the gang at age 13 and has been heavily involved in gang activities since then. Yolanda has sold drugs and participated in other crimes, including violent crimes. Yolanda has been arrested more than 25 times. She is a leader of the female members of the Hoover Crips in her neighborhood. Yolanda claims to have participated in a number of gang shoot-outs, and has the proof in arrests and wounds. She has worked a number of jobs, including one at the airport. She claims to attend church every once in a while and would choose her family over her gang, if forced to make the choice.

At 16 Tina was proud of her membership in the Downtown Westside Chicas and Chicos. The gang had only been active in her southern Colorado city for a little over a year. Tina had been one of the two females and five males who started the gang. The male leader of the gang had been a gang member in California before he moved to Tina's community. He was Tina's boyfriend and the father of her 14-month-old daughter. Tina and her fellow members held that their gang had been formed to protect the youth in their neighborhood from gangs from other neighborhoods. Since its formation the gang had grown in size and activity. Tina dropped out of school in the eighth grade when she was pregnant. She felt that she spent too much time with the gang instead of with her daughter. She said that she didn't feel right taking her baby with her to gang activities or dressing her in gang colors as some the other young mothers in the gang did. Tina's goals in life were to return to school, get a job, get married, move from the dangerous east side of the city to the safer south side, and have one more baby, a boy. Four months after Tina was interviewed as part of a research study (when her daughter would have been 18-months-old), Tina was killed in an automobile accident. Eight youths were in the car. All were alleged to have been drinking beer and "huffing" (inhaling) paint. Though five others were hospitalized, only Tina died. Her 14-year-old sister continued to be a member of the gang.

There was little interest in female gang members prior to the 1980s, when interest in females in gangs began to grow. In the 1990s interest in gang involvement by females has virtually exploded. An abundance of media stories, in print and on television, and at least one major motion picture are complemented by a growing body of research by journalists as well as social scientists. In this chapter, we discuss the issue of female gang involvement by:

- Examining the limited criminal justice statistics on the level of female gang involvement

- Reviewing common misconceptions about female gang involvement that resulted from a male-centered research focus

- Identifying central themes in ongoing research on female gang involvement

- Briefly linking these themes to available research results

We frame our discussion around three research examples that we feel have shaped research on female gang involvement:

- Frederic Thrasher's study of predominantly male gangs in early 20th-century Chicago

- Anne Campbell's research on female gang members in New York City in the early 1980s

- Joan Moore's research on females involved in East Los Angeles gangs over a period spanning several decades

These examples are only a small part of a growing body of research on female gang involvement. We also refer to other research in discussing the impact of these three examples. Readers who have a greater interest in female involvement should to seek out the numerous studies cited in this chapter.

Measuring the Scope of Female Gang Involvement

National-level estimates of the scope and magnitude of gang problems were addressed in Chapter 1. As noted there, national-level surveys have sought to assess the scope and magnitude of gang problems. Several of these surveys looked at the issue of gang involvement and gender. Here we review what these studies show about female involvement in gangs. That is to say, examining how law enforcement agencies portray female gang involvement.

The Number of Female Gang Members

From the first national survey of gang problems, Walter Miller (1975, p. 23) proposed as a "general estimate" that 10 percent or less of the gang members in the cities that he studied were female. In no cities did Miller actually find a reported 10 percent of gang members who were females. For Chicago, the estimate was "almost" 10 percent. The New York City Police Department estimated that half of their city's male gangs had female auxiliaries, yet estimated females to account for only 6 percent of all gang members. In any case, Miller's estimate has remained a rule of thumb in estimating the level of female gang involvement (Spergel, 1990). No recent studies of police data on gang members have approached the 10 percent estimate. In the 1988 National Gang Survey, the estimate of female gang members obtained from 34 cities was just under 4 percent. From the 1992 national survey, only 3.7 percent of gang members on which 61 police jurisdictions maintained official records were female. In terms of raw numbers, the number of female gang members reported by law enforcement *has* increased over three national surveys that have been interested in the issue. From the 34 police agencies responding to the 1988 National Gang Survey, an estimate of 4,803 female gang members was computed. Sixty-one police agencies reporting to the 1992 NIJ National Gang Survey reported 9,092 female gang members (see Figure 5-1).

To suggest that the estimates and statistics on female gang members provided by law enforcement are accurate representations of female gang involvement would be careless. Researchers including Meda Chesney-Lind, Randall Shelden, and Karen Joe (1996) have argued that earlier researchers and police have had "gendered habits." In other words, these critics argued that females had been as invisible as gang members as they had historically been invisible as

Figure 5-1
Jurisdictions Reporting Female Gang Members in 1992
1992 NIJ NAtional Gang Survey

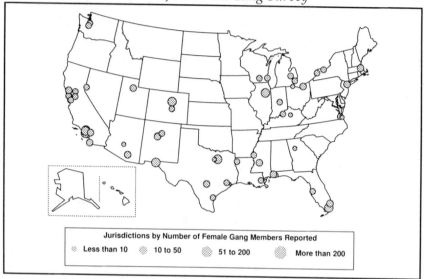

Jurisdictions by Number of Female Gang Members Reported

Less than 10   10 to 50   51 to 200   More than 200

potential crime- and fire-fighters. Evidence for this conclusion was found in the results of the 1992 National Gang Survey (Curry, Ball, and Fox, 1994). Some cities reported that as a matter of policy, females were not counted as gang members. A few cities only counted females as "associate gang members." In all, 32 percent of police departments with reported gang crime problems did not keep statistics on female gang members. Nine more would have reported female gang members had any been known to be involved in gangs in their jurisdictions. These nine felt confident in reporting no female gang members.

Gang Crimes by Females

The 1992 National Gang Survey (Curry, Ball, and Fox, 1994a) asked police departments for information on the numbers of gang-related crimes by crime type and gender of offender. From the limited number of jurisdictions that provided this information, comparisons were made between gang crimes committed by male and female members. As noted above, the "rule" of attributing 10 percent of gang problems to women has never held up for national censuses of gang members. Controlling for availability of data, the 10 percent rule may be a good one for levels of gang-related crimes, however. For each type of crime except gang-related homicides, gang-related crimes with female offenders exceed 10 percent. Males committed far more offenses over all. Figure 5-2 shows the differences between males and females in kinds of gang crimes committed. A greater portion of gang-related crimes by males were violent in nature, while a greater share of gang-related crimes by females were property crimes.

Independent/Autonomous Female Gangs

Walter Miller (1975, p. 23) classified female gangs into three types: (1) female auxiliary gangs affiliated with male gangs, (2) mixed-sex gangs with both male and female members, and (3) independent or autonomous female gangs. His results suggested that in the 1970s and 1980s, the most common of these types was the female auxiliary to a male gang. Without doubt, the rarest of gangs involving females were independent, autonomous female gangs. Miller found only one autonomous female gang in New York City

Figure 5-2
Proportion of Gang Offenses by Type and by Gender
(Available Data) 1992 NIJ National Survey

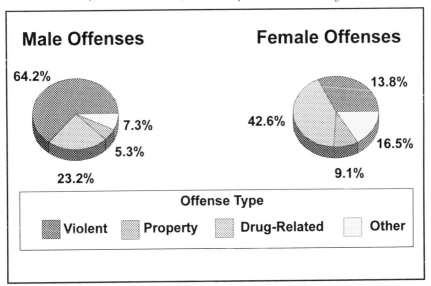

in 1975. By 1982, Miller (1982, p. 74) reported six autonomous female gangs in the Bronx and Queens. There were few more in other locations. The 1988 National Youth Gang Survey tabulated reports of 22 "independent" female gangs. The 1992 NIJ national survey received reports of 99 independent female gangs spread over 35 law enforcement jurisdictions in 1991. The distribution of independent female gangs in 1992 is shown in the map in Figure 5-3.

Thrasher and the Male-Centered View of Females and Gangs

In this text, we label as "myths" propositions that stand in opposition to the weight of evidence compiled by research. Some of the myths about female gangs come from the work of respected gang researchers. Primary among these is Frederic Thrasher. Thrasher's conclusions about female gang involvement legitimized beliefs that dominated views of female gang involvement for decades.

As we have shown in other chapters, research about gangs has been going on for most of the 20th century. To a more limited extent, this is also true about female involvement in gangs. Frederic

Figure 5-3
Jurisdictions Reporting at Least One Independent Female Gang
1992 NIJ National Gang Survey

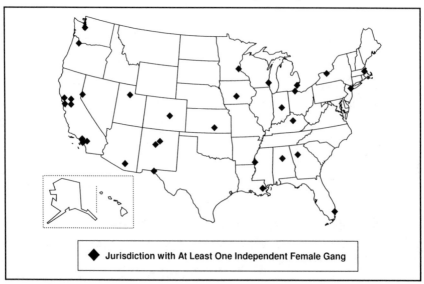

◆ Jurisdiction with At Least One Independent Female Gang

Thrasher (1927) was a former probation officer who became a student of sociology at the University of Chicago. As a graduate student, Thrasher pursued a fascination with gangs that he had developed during his work with the delinquent youth of Chicago. While most of Thrasher's study of 1,313 Chicago gangs focused on male gang involvement, he did say some things about females and gangs that would become a basis for much of what others who came after him would also observe. Many of his observations are now considered to be the result of male biases that were then pervasive in universities and society at large.

Thrasher: 'Girls Do Not Form or Participate in Gangs'

From his perspective, Thrasher believed that females simply did not form or participate in gangs. He even gave some consideration that there was some sort of "ganging instinct" that was found among males but not among females. Ultimately, though, Thrasher (p. 161) concluded that the reasons that females did not participate in gangs were social rather than biological. Based on his observations, Thrasher identified two social factors that he believed prevented females from being involved in gangs in the ways that males were. First, he believed that there were "traditions" and "customs" deeply rooted in society that instilled different values and norms for social behavior in females than in males. In contemporary delinquency theory, this perspective is very similar to one that has been labeled a subculture of gender. It is rooted in studies in anthropology and social psychology that have found that females are imbued with different values than males. For some, these differing values, specifically a greater tendency to altruism and caring about the needs of others, are functional to women's bearing a larger role in the nurture of children.

A second social factor that Thrasher thought to be important to females' not participating in gangs was the greater parental supervision of females in comparison to males. According to Thrasher, in the "urban disorganized areas" where gangs flourished, young males were subjected to less supervision than young males in more stable communities. Even in such "disorganized" communities, young females were much more closely supervised and guarded than young males, even in the same families. Females were also more likely to be involved in daily activities and responsibilities inside the home, while males were given the free, unsupervised time that made gang involvement possible. This observation by Thrasher that the greater parental supervision of females results in greater levels of delinquent behavior in males is a central proposition in the theory of delinquency known as power control theory.

According to Thrasher (p. 151), in the fairly uncommon instances when females were involved in gangs, they were younger females. He used the term "tomboy" to describe these females. Generally, their roles in gangs were the same as those taken by younger males. This kind of gang involvement by females was pictured as short-lived and passing. Puberty drove a wedge between these females and the predominantly male-dominated gangs in which this kind of involvement occurred. As Thrasher (p. 161) put it, "They took the roles of boys until they began to wear their hair up and put on long skirts."

Thrasher: 'The Only Roles That Females Play in Gangs Are as Objects of Sexual Exploitation and Manipulation by Male Gang Members'

When older females were involved in gangs, Thrasher (pp. 155, 164–66) described their role as explicitly sexual. Females were described by male gang members in terms of their capacity for sexual exploitation rather than any aspect of their personalities or other contributions to gang activities. In support of this allegation of sexual exploitation, Thrasher provided examples of female participation in "orgiastic" or "immoral" gangs. He emphasized that these orgiastic gangs were not true conflict groups and not a central part of the ganging behavior in which he was interested. For the true conflict gangs he studied, even sexual exploitation was a more occasional than regular behavior. Most common among these occasional conflict gang contacts with females described by Thrasher were "stag" parties where female nude dancers would perform. Male gang members often regaled Thrasher with accounts of "gang shags." A gang shag was an encounter in which multiple gang members would engage in sex with the same female. Thrasher described the gang as taking "certain girls" "under its protection" in the capacity of these sexual encounters. No specific details, however, were provided about the ways in which these females were actually protected.

In spite of his general representation of the gang as the realm of males, Thrasher tentatively entertained an idea about liberation that ran contrary to most of his other observations. As did "liberal feminist" theorists in the 1970s, Thrasher (p. 168) considered the possibility that changes in the structure of sex roles in society could have an impact on female involvement in delinquent activity, including participation in gangs. In his words, "Since the occupations of men, formerly closed to women, have been opened to them, what is inconsistent about their entering the time-honored profession of the highwayman?" To establish the validity of his considering such a possibility, Thrasher presented an account of a female gang member, "Honey," who took a leadership role in a "bandit gang" (See Box 5-1). Thrasher did not display a lot of confidence in the liberation idea or the woman's account of events. Following the presentation, he noted that it was more likely that the woman played more of a "brains" role than that of the fighting leader typical of gangs. He also suggested that the main activity of the gang was burglary rather than robbery.

Thrasher: 'The Major Relationship of Females to Gangs Is as "Destroyers" of the Gang by Encouraging Male Gang Members to Marry and Take Jobs'

For Thrasher, females played their most significant role for the gang from their position outside the gang. Females held a position in the lives of adolescent males that made them the greatest threat to the collectivity and solidarity that was the basis of gang life as described by Thrasher. As he put it, as the gang member grew older, "sex got more attention." He did not mean sexual exploitation. He was referring to what he called "the biological function of sex." In this function, sex was associated with love, marriage, and family formation. To the degree that it was associated with love and marriage, sex was for Thrasher (p. 170) "the chief disintegrating force in the gang." Marriage brought the imposition of family structures, responsibilities, and relationships. The male who was lured away from the family by the attractive excitement of the gang peer group was in the end usually lured back into the institution of the family by individual females as wives. In Thrasher's words, "The gang which once supplanted the home, now succumbs to it. . . ."

Box 5-1

A diminutive, bobbed-haired girl of twenty-one, who thrilled with pride on being told she resembled Clara Phillips, the hammer-slayer, but wept with shame at the thought of bringing sadness to her mother, last night confessed to the Evanston police that she was the brains and sometimes the brawn of a bandit crew responsible for seventy-five North Shore robberies and holdups.

____ ____ is her name, but she particularly requested that it be given as "Honey," explaining that that was what "the fellows" called her. In jail with her is ____ ____, while Tom is out on $2,000 bonds, being named by Honey as her crime lieutenants. Glen ____ whom she coyly terms her sheik; Connie ____ and Roy ____ are sought.

Honey mingled her story with many a "My Gawd!" and "That's the hell of it!" and resentfully explained that her arrest came when a "bunch of those damn police overheard me telling about one of the jobs I pulled."

"My gang didn't have the nerve, that was the trouble. My sheik, Glen, was O.K., but I had to steer him. But that was yellow. One night we were waiting to pull a stick at Ridge and Dempster and he got cold feet. I stuck my gun to his head and said:

"'I'll blow your brains out if you try to quit now.'

"That brought him across all right.

"Glen started me on this stuff, I guess. I worked in my mother's confectionery store. I'd go out with him and sit in the car while he pulled stickups, but he didn't know how to work them, so I took charge. Then we annexed the rest of the gang and put over some swell jobs."

Genevieve Forbes, "Girl, Twenty-one, Tells How She Ruled Holdup Gang," *Chicago Tribune*, January 3, 1923.

Campbell Discovers the Females in the Gang

Without doubt, the publication of Anne Campbell's (1984, 2nd ed. 1991) *The Girls in the Gang* marked a turning point in how researchers thought about females and gangs. We must note that at least three valuable studies on female gang members had been published prior to Campbell's book. Each of the works of these three male researchers preceded Campbell in transcending the male-centered stereotypes found in Thrasher's work. Walter Miller (1973) reported the results of his study of two female gangs, one white, the Molls, and one African American, the Queens, in the 1950s and 1960s; Waln Brown (1977) recorded the gang-related activity of African American females in Philadelphia; and John Quicker (1983) studied Chicana involvement in gangs in southern California. The findings of each reveal females participating in gang activity that is to some degree independent of that of the male gangs with whom they associated. However, none of these three studies received as much attention as *The Girls in the Gang*.

A junior professor at Rutgers University, Campbell wanted to "write a book about young women by a woman." She stressed that this was important since most research in the social sciences had previously been limited by being "about men and by men." She felt that this had especially been the case for research on gangs. Truly understanding social phenomenon, Campbell argued, required vicariously experiencing "its lived reality" through the eyes of its participants. In order to come into contact with female gang members, she relied on two gatekeepers. The first was Sergeant John Galea of the New York Police Department's gang unit. Through his cordial street relationships with gang girls, Galea introduced Campbell to gang members. Her second gatekeeper was a former gang member, Nazim Fatah, who ran a not-for-profit group, the Inner City Roundtable of Youth, that worked with active gang members to find them jobs and to resolve intergang conflicts. Campbell worked as a volunteer newsletter editor for the Roundtable, and eventually, through her two initial contacts and her own continued presence in the community, made contact with the gang members that she felt to be most representative of the diversity of gang life as she encountered it.

The core of Campbell's completed effort was three social biographies, each a portrait of a woman involved in a different female gang in New York City. She worked with each from 1979 into the early 1980s. The first of the women profiled by Campbell (pp. 49–105) was Connie. In her early 30s, Connie was Puerto Rican and a mother of four. Connie's gang was the Sandman Ladies. The Sandman Ladies were the female auxiliary gang of the Sandman. The Sandman was identified by police as a Manhattan drug-selling gang. Campbell emphasized the Sandman's aspirations of being a motorcycle club, though as she admitted she had observed the gang in possession of only one working motorcycle during the time of her study. For each of her three subjects, Campbell attempted to "reconstruct" their social biographies. In Connie's biography, Campbell devoted a great deal of attention to Connie's efforts to be a good mother and be a part of the gang, which for her was a form of extended family. Connie expressed a desire that her children would have a life similar to her own in the gang. She adorned her children in gang colors and symbols, complemented by photographs, including one of her toddler in the garb of a "Sandman Tot." While violence and the gang's marijuana-selling operation were given less attention by Campbell, their importance to Connie's day-to-day existence could not be ignored. At one point it was stressed that to be a Sandman Lady, a girl had to be willing to fight. Campbell's contact with Connie was at one point broken for a long period of time while as a result of gang-related killings and threats on the lives of her and her children she went into hiding.

Campbell's (pp. 106–75) second reconstructed biography was of Weeza. Weeza was also Puerto Rican, in her late 20s, and a mother of two. Weeza was a member of the Sex Girls (originally the Essex Girls, named after Essex street). The Sex Girls were the female auxiliary gang of the Sex Boys. The Sex Boys had also gotten their name from their Essex street turf. In Campbell's opinion, of the gangs she studied, the Sex Boys and Girls corresponded most to "the classic New York street gang." She described the gang as being in the final stages of disintegration at the time of her research. Heavy police suppression and rivalries with neighboring gangs had taken their tolls on the gang. Based on police arrest records, the gang had an eight-year history characterized by violence, robbery, and auto theft. Most of the gang activity that Campbell observed involved drug use and petty sales. Descriptions of violence by males and females was mostly retrospective. The central theme in Campbell's account of Weeza is of Weeza's life with her live-in boyfriend Popeye and their children. Most of the gang members were trying unsuccessfully to complete drug treatment programs and obtain legitimate jobs. Weeza's story ended with the poignant description of the execution-style murder of Popeye.

The third subject of Campbell's (pp. 176–231) biographies was Sun-Africa. Sun-Africa was an African-American teenager whose parents had immigrated to New York City from Panama shortly before she was born. At the time of Campbell's research, Sun-Africa was a member of the Five Percenters. The Five Percenters were a self-described religious (Islamic) and cultural movement. In contrast, the New York Police Department described them as a gang with a history of criminal activity dating back to the early 1960s. Sun-Africa was different from Campbell's other subjects in that she provided Campbell with descriptions of two very different experiences in two very different gangs. In her first period of gang involvement, Sun-Africa had been a member of an independent female gang called the Puma Crew. Sun-Africa reported experiencing problems with school discipline at a very young age. She told Campbell that she had begun smoking marijuana at age 8 and "fooling around" with boys shortly thereafter. When she was 11, she had joined the Puma Crew. Most of the Puma Crew were younger girls and their delinquency was limited to drug use and fist-fighting. Shortly after she turned 14, she and the other members of the Puma Crew began to hang out with male members of the Five Percenters. She ran away from home, participated in burglaries and shoplifting, and continued her marijuana use. One of her boyfriends was killed in an attempted robbery. Her brother was wounded and subsequently sent to prison as a result of the same incident. The event had a profound effect on her. Shortly thereafter, at age 15, Sun-Africa became seriously involved with the Five Percenters. In contrast to the independence associated with being a member of the all-female Puma Crew, full participation in the Five Percenters required her to accept the teachings of Islam as practiced by the group. For her as a female, this meant accepting her role as a subordinate to males and behaving as a good Moslem woman. Each female who entered the Five Percenter Nation had to be accepted and ruled over by a male group member, referred to as her "god." When Campbell interviewed her, she was leading a life of docility and servitude under the care of her second god since joining the group. Still, she spent most of her life in a collective dwelling with other women of the group, while their gods visited on rare occasions.

Campbell: 'Females Become Involved in Gangs and Illegitimate Activities Through Relationships With Male Gang Members'

From her research, Campbell (p. 32) arrived at two major conclusions about female gang involvement. We will examine the two conclusions separately. The first conclusion was that males play a major role in getting females involved in gangs and gang-related crime. In Campbell's wording, "It is still the male gang that paves the way for the female affiliate and opens the door into many illegitimate opportunities and into areas that serve as proving grounds." This conclusion has import on more than one level. On an individual basis, many females become involved in gangs through relationships with boyfriends or brothers. This was certainly the case for the females who were the subjects of Campbell's three case studies. Again, on an individual level, this also suggests that female members of mixed-sex gangs become involved in delinquent or criminal activity through their association with the males in the gang. On a collective level, this conclusion also suggests that female gang auxiliaries, through their association with male gangs, become involved in delinquent and criminal activity. Of Campbell's two conclusions, this one has inspired little debate.

Campbell: 'For Females, Gang Membership Can Be Liberating by Involving Them in a Sisterhood and Providing Them With a Sense of Solidarity and Self-Actualization'

It is Campbell's second major conclusion that has generated debate among others who have researched female gang involvement. Campbell concluded that once a female is involved in gangs, "a more visible solidarity or 'sisterhood' within the gang appears. A girl's status depends to a larger extent on her female peers." Rank and worth within the gang is not a matter of relationships with males or "simple sexual attractiveness." This conclusion suggests that for females in the gang, there are opportunities for self-actualization and equality not available to them in other ways. In other words, gang participation is for females a path to liberation. This theme is one that has had great appeal for journalists, some of whom have gone so far as to describe female gang members as "street feminists" (LeBlanc, 1994). Meda Chesney-Lind (1993) characterized these ideas as the "liberation hypothesis."

Moore's Research on Gender and Gang Involvement

Joan Moore (1991) produced a study that was unique in a number of ways. First, Moore used a random sample of a large population of gang members who had been contacted during an earlier multiple-year project. Almost all prior studies of gang members had depended on purposive, opportunity, or snowball samples. In addition to relying on random selection, Moore's sample of 156 respondents was large in comparison to most studies using in-depth interviews. The study was restricted to two multigenerational barrio gangs located in two different East Los Angeles communities. Second, Moore's sample included two generations of gang members. An older portion (40 percent) of her sample had joined their gangs in the late 1940s and early 1950s. The remainder or younger group joined their gangs in the 1960s and 1970s. Third and most important for the current chapter, one-third of Moore's interviewees were female gang members. All were interviewed in 1985 and all were adults.

Moore used what she has called the "collaborative" model of research. The essence of this model is that the researcher works collaboratively with community residents who have been gang members. Interview formats and questions to be asked in interviews are developed in cooperation with individuals who come from the same social context and experiences as the interviewees. These community researchers learn about the research, contribute to it, assist in its conduct, and develop a sense of ownership toward it. The in-depth interviews conducted by Moore and her community collaborators were systematic and open-ended. The same range of questions were covered in each interview, but those being interviewed could expand on their answers and even criticize the limitations of the questions asked. Subjects covered included the interviewees' knowledge of the gang, their personal experiences with the gang, their family and adolescent peer experiences, and the processes for leaving the gang.

Within the two larger gang umbrellas were many age-graded groups called "cliques" (klikas). The female gang members interviewed in Moore's study (pp. 27–31) belonged to cliques that varied in their relationships to male cliques. Some female members were integrated into mixed-sex cliques. Others belonged to cliques that were closely tied to male cliques. Still others were relatively independent of any specific male cliques. In some cliques, Moore found that female members were more likely to be girlfriends of male gang members. In others, the female members were almost all relatives of male gang members. Moore (p. 29) described one comparatively autonomous female clique in which most of the members had older sisters who had been in an older clique of the same gang name.

While she found that activities varied from clique to clique, Moore found a number of parallel behaviors among female and male gang members. The older generations of gang members were less likely to report initiation rituals as a way of entering the gang. Moore (p. 59) concluded, though, that jumping in rituals had become more common and more important for "boys and girls" who had joined their cliques more recently. In a "jumping in" ritual, a new member is required to stand up to a beating by other members of the gang. The female gang members often recounted participation in violence. One woman recalled how her female sisters and cousins in her gang had encouraged her to engage in fights from a very early age. Moore (p. 59) suggested that gang violence has become more serious over time. Older gang members spoke about fistfights, but younger gang members, both male and female, were more likely to talk of guns. As in most other studies of gang members, Moore (p. 50) found that gang members, male and female, spent a considerable amount of time hanging out and partying. Though less so for females than for males, a central part of hanging out and partying was "drinking or getting high."

In their descriptions of the circumstances that led to their joining the gang, females were more likely than males to draw Moore's (p. 48) attention to family problems. Still, family relationships were important, in that "women were more likely to mention problems at home when they talked about joining the gang." Moore also points out that females in the gang "were notably more likely to have run away from home than boys." Three-quarters of the female members with whom Moore (p. 99) spoke reported running away from home at least once. Of the female gang members, 45 percent grew up with a heroin addict in the home compared to 20 percent of the males. A member of their family had been arrested during their childhood for 82 percent of the females and for 57 percent of the males (p. 101). Though 29 percent of Moore's female interviewees reported being victims of incest, Moore felt that this statistic was not significantly higher than that for nongang females. From her interviews, Moore (p. 79) concluded that problems in school were not linked to gang membership. Friends and associates outside the gang were uncommon for all of the gang members interviewed by Moore (p. 50), but contacts outside the gang were even less common for younger female gang members.

Moore: 'The Social Harms Associated With Female Gang Membership Outweigh Any Social or Psychological Benefits'

To some extent, Moore's findings supplemented and supported those of Campbell. Moore, however, took explicit objection to Campbell's version of the liberation proposition. Moore (p. 55) charged that Campbell's assertion of sisterhood and solidarity amounted to an argument that "gang girls have outgrown their sexist image." To speak of liberation in a new sisterhood and solidarity for females in gangs was unacceptable for Moore in the social world of gangs, in which she found extreme levels of practiced and professed sexism. Despite protestations to the contrary from many of the female gang members, Moore discovered that a significant number of male gang members thought of their female compatriots as sexual possessions. Moore (p. 54) identified three basic sets of ideas about females prevalent among male gang members:

The gang is a male preserve where women don't belong.

Male dominance of females is natural and legitimate.

As a greater good for the higher needs of the group, embattled male gang warriors require the sexual use of females.

Sexist attitudes and behavior were not a province limited to males. In many cases, females supported or engaged in the sexual exploitation of their "sisters." Moore (pp. 55–56) offered an account provided by a female gang member in which all female members of one gang showed up in court to support a homeboy accused of rape by one of their homegirls. Their purpose, according to the girl, was to assist the male gang member's defense lawyer to make the rape victim "look like a tramp." Sexist attitudes did not show any evidence of becoming less common among gang members in the more recent gang generations studied by Moore.

More important to Moore than the pervasive sexism that she found in gangs has been her belief that the harms associated with gang involvement for females simply outweigh any benefits. She has contended that gang membership has more long-term harmful effects on females than on male gang members. Female gang members were more likely than male gang members to be responsible for rearing their children (p. 114). The children of female gang members were significantly more likely than the children of male gang members to become gang members themselves. Through this greater impact of gang membership on their children alone, Moore has suggested that the ultimate harm done to community and society may be greater for females than for males.

Research Findings and Issues in Female Gang Involvement

Level of Involvement

The numbers of female gang members reported and the crimes attributed to them by police in national surveys consistently increased over the last decade. Field research on female gangs has likewise increased. Very few researchers would currently suggest that females don't form or participate in gangs. Thrasher's concern about why females don't participate in gangs might be restated to the question, why don't females participate in gangs as much as males? Finn-Aage Esbensen and David Huizinga reported that 25 percent of gang members identified in their Denver survey were females. As noted above, Joan Moore estimated that one-third of the gang members that she studied were females. Meda Chesney-Lind and her co-authors have supported those who argue that female participation in gangs continues to be underestimated.

There is another alternative to the nonparticipation myth. In comparison to male gang involvement, it just may be that female gang involvement is not serious enough to be considered a problem. In 1995, two overviews of gang problems by senior researchers minimized the significance of the female gang problem. Malcolm Klein (1995, pp. 111–12) pointed out that females were identified as suspects in only 2 percent of 1,346 Los Angeles County gang-related homicides. Of 631 Chicago gang homicide offenders, three were females. This led Irving Spergel (1995, p. 58) to conclude that gang violence was "essentially a male problem." In terms of general delinquency, the interaction between gang membership and gender may still require special attention. Jeffrey Fagan (1990) found that female gang members reported higher levels of delinquency than male nongang members.

Sexual Exploitation of Female Gang Members

Sexual exploitation or attempts at sexual exploitation of female gang members have been reported by a range of studies. The role of women in the Five Percent Nation described by Anne Campbell (1984/1991) was clearly a sexually submissive one. (See Box 5-2.) As noted above, the sexism observed by Moore (1991) led her to reject

Box 5-2
Six Rules of the Black Woman
(From "Lessons" of the Five Percent Nation in Campbell 1991, p.220)

1. The black woman is not to sell her physical composition for any payment.
2. The black woman is not to tamper with the god's (male's) star by using any form of birth control.
3. The black woman is not to have emotional affects with anyone but her man, regardless if they are devoted to ISLAM.
4. The black woman is to keep and obey the rules and regulation given by her man.
5. The black woman must reflect the light of god and reflect it on her star (child).
6. The black woman must make sure her womb and vagina is clean before permitting her man to plant his seed in her vagina.

the images of liberation offered by Campbell. Moore described the less prevalent, but still existent, support of sexist standards among the female gang members. Laura Fishman (1995) described sexual exploitation as a major part of the female gang involvement that she observed among the Vice Queens, a female auxiliary gang that she studied in Chicago. The Vice Queens were available for sex upon request by the male members of their male gang counterparts, the Vice Kings. More so, Fishman portrayed Vice Queens as serving as prostitutes to raise funds for the Vice Kings. In some cases, Vice Queens even conceived and bore children upon the request of their Vice King counterparts. In a 1990s study of female gang members in Ohio, Jody Miller (1996) described sexist attitudes among female gang members and incidents of sexual exploitation in mixed-sex gangs.

The weakness of the description of sexual exploitation offered by Thrasher was its emphasis on sexual exploitation as the "only" role for older girls in gangs. As presented, the idea can be dismissed if either of two kinds of evidence emerge from research on female gang involvement. The first would be evidence of gangs where female members experience no sexual exploitation. The second would be gangs in which female members have nonsexual roles. Walter Miller (1973) studied two female gangs, the Molls and the Queens. Waln Brown (1977) studied female gang members in independent and mixed-sex gangs in Philadelphia. Quicker (1983) and Harris (1988) conducted separate studies of Chicana gang members in California female auxiliary gangs. In none of these gangs were female members sexually available to their male gang counterparts. In Ruth Horowitz's (1983) study of Chicago Mexican-American gangs, the same cultural norms that prevented females from engaging in gang activity also served to provide a level of protection against blatant sexual exploitation. The evidence against sexual exploitation as the *only* role of females within gangs is more prevalent. As noted above, both Campbell and Moore described females as active participants in gang violence. Spergel (1963) and Fishman (1988, 1995) reported females participating in gang conflicts as spies and weapons bearers. Fishman reported them engaging in independent intergang violence with other female gangs. From a survey study of male and female gang members, Fagan (1990, p. 213) concluded, "Females in gangs appear to be involved extensively in versatile patterns of illegal behaviors."

Decker and Van Winkle (1996, p. 72) noted that the greatest variation in reported sexual exploitation of female gang members as reported by St. Louis gang members was associated with gender. Reports
of females submitting to serial intercourse with male gang members
as part of initiation to membership were exclusively attributed to male
interviewees. None of the female gang members interviewed in St.
Louis reported having undergone such an initiation, and none reported ever knowing any woman who had.

In an ironic twist on the sexual exploitation proposition, David
Lauderback, Joy Hansen, and Dan Waldorf (1992) described the exploitation of females by an autonomous and independent female gang,
the Protrero Posse. In their lucrative crack cocaine operation, the Posse
encouraged the presence of females who provided sexual favors in
exchange for crack at their crack houses. That female gang members
should sexually exploit other females is certainly not in keeping with
the sexual exploitation myth.

Females as 'Destroyers' of the Gang

Do women play the major role in pulling males away from
gangs? In his study of the Nortons, a male gang in Boston, William
F. Whyte (1943) recounted how an alliance between the gang and
an independent female group, the Aphrodite Club, ultimately
changed the social organization of the gang and drew members
away from the gang. The great bulk of the research literature on
female gang involvement has shown females as supporters and perpetrators of the gang. This was especially the case in Horowitz's
(1983) and Moore's (1991) studies of Mexican-American gang members in Chicago and Los Angeles. Spergel (1964) described female
gang involvement in terms of their support of male gang conflicts.
Female associates carried "tales" that fanned the flames of intergang
hostilities. By carrying and hiding weapons for males, females
played a more obvious support role. Research in the 1980s and 1990s
on the male populations most at risk of gang involvement has emphasized the unavailability of jobs for inner-city minority males.
William Julius Wilson (1987, 1996) has identified the declining pool
of "marriageable" males in poor communities. Hagedorn (1988) described how Wilson's concept of marriageable males applied especially to gang members. If females ever sought to pull gang members

away from gangs, they must be less likely to do so in the face of the declining "value" of male gang members as viable partners.

Relationships With Males and Female Gang Involvement

The male influence proposition had strong support in both the work of Campbell and Moore. The link between Walter Miller's (1973) Queens and crime ran through their male counterpart gang the Kings. The independent female gang studied by Lauderback and his colleagues (1992) was said to have learned the crack trade from former boyfriends. Hagedorn and Devitt (1997, p. 13) have argued that focusing on the relationship between female gang members and male gang members perpetuates the tradition of male bias in studying female gang involvement.

Liberation and Female Gang Membership

Campbell was not the first to propose the independent role of females in gangs. Miller (1973) noted that the female members in the Boston gang the Molls were not controlled by the members of their male affiliate gang and that their leadership consisted of a subset of female members. The Holly Hos studied by Brown (1977) in Philadelphia were autonomous from any male gang. Even among the mixed-sex gangs studied by Brown, female members attained their own individual status positions based on their contributions to the gang. Quicker (1983) studying Chicana gangs concluded that these gangs were auxiliaries to male gangs, but he also described decision making within the female gangs to be democratic and decentralized. He observed only limited efforts by the affiliated male gangs to control the female groups. Mary Harris (1988), in a subsequent study of Chicana gangs, found partial support for the independence of female cliques observed by Quicker. As noted below, though, Harris also reported efforts by male gang members to sexually exploit and control the female gang members with which they were associated. Of gang members in St. Louis interviewed by Decker and Van Winkle (1994, 1996; Decker, 1996), 70 percent reported that the roles of males and females in their gangs were indistinguishable. These roles were selling drugs, shooting, fighting, and stealing.

While most researchers who found support for liberation in gang membership didn't go so far as Campbell in advocating the position, there have been two exceptions. As noted above, a team of San Francisco researchers (Lauderback, Hansen, and Waldorf, 1992) described the activities of the Potrero Hill Posse. The posse was described as "a strictly independent group of young African American women." The major profit-making activity of the gang was a well-organized operation for dealing crack cocaine. A similar portrait of female gang involvement in drug trafficking was provided by Carl Taylor (1993) from his research in Detroit. Taylor's work marks him as one of the strongest supporters of the liberation proposition. Taylor (p. 10) attributed "a new attitude of female criminal independence" among female gang members to their participation in gangs and drug selling. Such involvement has in his words (p. 23) "empowered" female gang members. In a review of what is known about female gang involvement, Chesney-Lind, Shelden, and Joe (1996) used Taylor's study as a case example in their critique of the liberation proposition as represented by the glorification of the "liberated female crook." Chesney-Lind and her colleagues argued that Taylor's conclusions were not supported by the portions of interviews with female gang members that he included in his book. From their analysis of his own interviews, Chesney-Lind argued that, rather than describing empowerment, Taylor's female gang interviewees were describing a gang world filled with sexism and social injury.

Social Harm and Female Gang Involvement

Among researchers who have emphasized social harm in comparison to liberation as an outcome of female gang involvement are Joan Moore (1991), Karen Joe, Meda Chesney-Lind (1995), and Jody Miller (1996). Related questions are, how do females who belong to gangs differ from other females and how do females who are involved in gangs differ from male gang members? Only a few studies have addressed these important questions. All of the examples to be discussed here are what are called quasi-experimental designs (Cook and Campbell, 1979). When a set of behaviors such as gang involvement cannot be studied under laboratory conditions, the only alternative is to study it in its natural social setting. Most field studies concentrate on learning as much as possible about any members of the group in which the researcher is interested. As researchers pay more attention to how subjects for study are selected, attempt to include individuals from clearly discernible groups, and use statistical methods, they move toward using quasi-experimental designs. All of these considerations begin to compensate for the scientific advantages of the laboratory and methods of random assignment found in true experiments. As we discuss each of the following studies, how quasi-experimental designs can be used to draw conclusions about social behavior should become more obvious.

One sophisticated quasi-experimental design used to study female gang members was reported before Campbell published *Girls in the Gang*. Lee Bowker and Malcolm Klein (1983) combined data from the juvenile justice system and from survey results to produce a research design that allowed several important comparisons. From the juvenile court, Bowker and Klein obtained data on females who had been identified as delinquent. To complement this sample of females adjudicated by the court, Bowker and Klein collected comparable data from a sample of females who lived in neighborhoods where gangs were known to be active. From this kind of design, Bowker and Klein were able to make comparisons between four categories of females. These were (1) female gang members adjudicated as delinquent by the court, (2) nongang females adjudicated as delinquent by the court, (3) female gang members with no court contacts, and (4) nongang females with no court contacts. The survey included several batteries of psychological tests. Using techniques of statistical analysis, Bowker and Klein were able to examine both social and psychological factors that might contribute to female involvement in gangs and delinquency. Their conclusion (pp. 750–51) was that "racism, sexism, poverty, and limited opportunity structures" were the most important determinants of gang membership and juvenile delinquency among the females. At the same time, they concluded that "personality variables, relations with parents, and problems associated with heterosexual behavior" played only "a relatively minor role" in such outcomes.

Jeffrey Fagan (1990) provided one of the first large systematic surveys of juveniles that included information on female gang involvement. Fagan collected information on high school students and dropouts from each of three cities—Chicago, Los Angeles, and San Diego. Males and females in each sample were predominantly African American and Latino/a. Gang members were identified by asking them whether or not they had ever been a member of a gang.

Fagan's research design allowed him to compare four kinds of youths. These included male gang members, male nongang members, female gang members, and female nongang members. Fagan measured delinquency with 12 items that asked youths whether or not they had committed specific delinquent acts. He found that gang members (male or female) were more likely to have reported victimization and substance abuse and have lower commitment to conventional values than nongang members. Female gang members had higher overall rates of delinquency than female nongang members. They did not, however, have rates of delinquency as high as those of male gang members. Female gang members had higher levels of family and social integration and lower levels of neighborhood integration than male gang members.

Quasi-experimental research designs are strengthened if the research is longitudinal. In a longitudinal study, information is gathered from or on the same individuals at different points in time. The Rochester Youth Development Study was a random survey of youth enrolled in the seventh and eighth grades in Rochester, New York. Over an 18-month period, each youth and an adult caretaker (in 95 percent of the cases, it was the mother or stepmother) were interviewed every six months. As with Fagan's research, gang involvement and delinquency were based on the young person's self-report. Beth Bjerregaard and Carolyn Smith (1993) used the Rochester data to examine differences across the four groups of male nongang members, male gang members, female nongang members, and female gang members. Thanks to the longitudinal nature of the data, Bjerregaard and Smith were able to show that increased delinquency and drug use were found for both males and females specifically during the periods when they reported being gang members. Females involved in gangs differed from those who were not in gangs in several ways. Female gang members were less successful in school than other females, had more delinquent peers than nongang females, and reported more sexual activity than nongang females. Bjerregaard and Smith were also interested in what differences might exist between the males and females who became gang members. For the most part, they found that the males and females who became gang members were very similar in terms of social background and reported experiences. The only major difference was that failing in school appeared to be a more important factor in gang involvement for females than for males.

Like the Bowker and Klein (1983) research discussed above, Karen Joe and Meda Chesney-Lind (1993), two professors at the University of Hawaii, used both official records and interviews with male and female juveniles to better understand the nature of gang involvement and gender. Joe and Chesney-Lind (p. 10) found the most common arrest category for female gang members was larceny theft. For male gang members the most common arrest category was "other assaults" ("most likely fighting"). Based on their study of gang members in Hawaii, Joe and Chesney-Lind rejected what they labeled the "liberation hypothesis" as a way of understanding female gang involvement. For them, gang involvement was not an act of rebellion but an attempt of "young women to cope with a bleak and harsh present as well as a dismal future."

If we regard higher levels of delinquency and the associated involvement with the juvenile justice system to be social injuries, the quasi-experimental studies reviewed here all stress the social injury associated with gang involvement for females. Field studies in addition to those of Moore have also supplemented the evidence of social injury. The results of Moore for Chicana gang involvement in Los Angeles are extremely similar to the observations of Ruth Horowitz (1983) who, as a graduate student at the University of Chicago, studied gangs in a Chicago Chicano community. Female participation in gangs was not the primary focus of Horowitz's research. Still, her attention to the cultural strains placed on maturing Chicana girls provided a sharp contrast with the greater emphasis on personal liberation found in Campbell's research. For females in the community studied by Horowitz (p. 13), the development of personal identity was constrained by the prevalent cultural symbols of "motherhood, virginity, and male domination." Horowitz (p. 133) reported female gangs that were both affiliated with male gangs and independent. In every case, however, female gang participation emerged as a form of (largely unsuccessful) struggle against male control. While a greater level of personal liberation and collective independence were reported by Mary Harris in her study of Chicana gangs in southern California, she reported that this was only accomplished over continued attempts by male gang members to dominate female gang members.

Summary

In this chapter, we have examined female involvement in gangs. First, we reviewed the available official data on the scope and magnitude of female involvement in gang related crime. Next we examined false perceptions of females and gangs that originated in early twentieth-century gang research and that still have a great deal of appeal for some representatives of the mass media. We showed how a number of these beliefs could be attributed to one of the most important gang researchers, Frederic Thrasher. Two examples of field research on female gang involvement were examined in some detail, the research on New York female gang members by Anne Campbell and research on Chicana gang members in East Los Angeles by Joan Moore. The work of Anne Campbell served as the foundation for what has been labeled the "liberation hypothesis," a label first used by Meda Chesney-Lind (1993). The research of Joan Moore emphasized the social harm associated with female gang involvement. Finally, we reviewed the relevance of other research on female gang involvement to the findings of Campbell and Moore. We feel that these debates continue to shape ongoing research on female gang involvement. A separate section on responding to female gang involvement is included in Chapter 8 of this book, where we discuss gang theory and policy.

Chapter Six

Gangs and Social Institutions

A key to understanding gang members is to place them in the broader context of the social institutions with which they interact and that help to shape their lives. In this chapter we place gang members in several key institutional contexts that have important implications for what they do, how they do it, and what their lives in and outside gangs are like. It is important to remember that all but the most hard core gang members lead a considerable portion of their lives outside gangs. Understanding what life is like in those settings is a key to developing a comprehensive picture of life in a gang. In this chapter we review five social institutions and their impact on the lives of gang members: (1) families, (2) schools, (3) the criminal justice system, (4) politics, and (5) the labor market.

Families

Appropriately, the first social institution we consider is the family, the first institution an individual interacts with. It is hard to overestimate the importance of the family in socializing young people, teaching them the rules of behavior in society, and taking the appropriate steps to keep them within those rules. Recent trends in the status of families in America, especially for the poorest residents of large cities, cause us to be concerned about the ability of the family to do its job in teaching and supervising youth.

Sociologist William Julius Wilson (1987) has documented the precipitous decline of the family, particularly among poor African American residents of large cities. He has linked this decline to the growth of the urban underclass, a group that experiences profound levels of concentrated poverty and social isolation. A growing number of children in these neighborhoods are growing up in female-headed families, which are the poorest in the nation. The declines in marriage and family formation, in Wilson's formulation, is a consequence of the increased rates of incarceration for African American males as well as the decline in their long-term employment prospects. Taken together, these conditions have reduced the desirability of marriage for many young women. One consequence of this condition is the lack of supervision for young children. As a consequence, many young children grow up with little or no direction, and the need for socialization and order in their lives is often found on the streets.

It is against this backdrop that gangs emerged in many cities. Many families were either under stress (Vigil, 1988) or lacked the resources, financial or emotional, to deal with threats to the welfare of their children. In many instances, gangs filled the void. The work of Joan Moore (1978; 1991) and James Diego Vigil (1988) in Los Angeles has pointed to the need for order and regulation in the lives of adolescents. Children naturally seek these conditions, and gangs have come to fulfill these needs for a growing number of youths. Just as the status of the family declined, gangs emerged and in many instances provided an alternative form of organization for the lives of young people. As a consequence, gangs have begun to fulfill many of the functions formerly held by the family. For example, gangs attract young men and women because they provide some degree of structure and activities that may otherwise be missing. Given their involvement in illegal activities, gangs are also a ready source of opportunities to make money. Finally, and perhaps most importantly, gangs provide social cohesion and status, two functions typically fulfilled by a working family.

This picture prompts us to ask the question, "Has the gang become a family?" This question is a natural extension of our argument in the preceding paragraph. Indeed, many gang members talk about their gang as if it were a family and use that exact term to describe the gang. Some commentators (Perkins, 1987; Brown, 1977) have argued that gangs are a natural extension of the African American family, the next step in the evolution of the African American experience in cities. Despite the weakened condition of the American family in many large cities, most gang members continue to be more committed to their natal families than to their gang.

A small body of research has asked gang members directly about the relative importance of gangs and the family. For example, Decker and Van Winkle (1994, 1996; Decker, 1996) learned from their sample of 99 active gang members that only one would choose the gang over the family if forced to make such a choice. These same authors and Diego Vigil also report that few gang members want their children to grow up to become gang members.

One of the emerging issues in the study of gangs and families is the intergenerational character of many gangs. As gangs proliferate and last longer, we have begun to see gang members become parents and raise children who are at risk for gang membership. This condition is most pronounced among the Chicano gangs of southern California, gangs that have become representatives of their culture. But African American gangs in cities like Chicago have been around long enough to see second- and even third-generation gang members within the same family. It is important to note that second- and third-generation gang members entered gangs for many of the same reasons their parents did; they were raised in neighborhoods with few social and economic opportunities and they were exposed to gang lifestyles on a daily basis. There is not a solid body of evidence to show that parents purposely encourage their offspring to become gang members by socializing them into the gang lifestyle. However, the condition of the family, especially in poor neighborhoods, will have important implications for the presence and power of gangs in urban and suburban neighborhoods.

Schools

After the family, schools are the most powerful socializing agent in the lives of adolescents. Children attend school every day (almost), interact with students from a variety of backgrounds, and influence each other in a variety of ways, both positive and negative. Schools have an important impact on the lives of gang and nongang members, providing the opportunity for nongang youth to learn about and become involved in gangs.

As pointed out above, the strength and stability of inner-city families have suffered as a result of national-level changes in the economy over the last two decades. The schools in those same communities have also experienced new pressures and problems. Just as strong families produce strong communities, strong communities have historically been associated with effective schools. This principle has an obvious converse. Weakened communities with struggling households produce schools that have a tenuous place in those communities and a limited capacity to prepare students for participation in mainstream society. The work of William Julius Wilson helps us in understanding how this weakening of families can be associated with an increased risk of gang involvement. Wilson's perceptions of the changing role of schools in these communities make it possible to extend our understanding of the institutional context of gang involvement to include schools as well as families. Wilson (1985, p. 37) has concluded that "a vicious cycle is perpetuated through the family, through the community, and through the schools."

In the vicious cycle portrayed by Wilson, schools fail communities and communities fail schools. Schools fail communities by not educating and graduating their students. Wilson (1985, 37–38) noted that in Chicago in the 1980s, more than half of the African American and Latino/a youths attending public schools dropped out before graduating. Of those graduating, less than half could read at or above the national average. The social isolation of families from the mainstream economy is paralleled by their isolation from their children's schools. In an extreme example, journalist Alex Kotlowitz (1991, p. 63) noted that at one time in Chicago's poor communities, school phone numbers weren't listed in phone books as a way of discouraging poorer African American parents from contacting their children's schools.

Communities fail schools by not providing a safe community environment in which teachers can teach and students can learn and by not providing school administrators with the fiscal or policy resources needed to overcome a growing host of problems. Again with his penchant for extreme examples, Kotlowitz (1991, p. 66) described how one Chicago teacher located her chair and desk behind a heavy pillar in order to reduce her risk of being shot from gunfire from the school's parking lot. In terms of the attention of policy makers, inner-city schools have suffered dramatically since the early 1980s. Jonathon Kozol (1991, p. 4), an outspoken activist for better public schools, has suggested that in the period in which the urban underclass has emerged, social policy on public schooling "has been turned back almost one hundred years." The issue that we examine here is how gangs fit into this pattern of mutual failure between school and communities.

Do Gangs Run Some Public Schools?

Some research supports the idea that gangs control certain public schools. Studies of gang problems across municipalities are extremely rare. An exception was part of Walter Miller's (1975, 1982) examination of the gang problem over the duration of his two national studies of youth gang crime. The Harvard anthropologist devoted chapters in both his 1975 and 1982 reports to gang activities in public schools. Based on his interviews with school officials, Miller (p. 46) argued that gangs were "operating *within* as well as outside" of schools in several of the nation's largest cities. His conclusion was that gangs posed "serious obstacles" to the education of students and "a serious threat to the physical safety of students and teachers." Miller (1982, pp. 131–132) suggested that an increase of school-based gangs in the 1970s was related to the weakened ability of schools to control students and a greater emphasis on keeping troublesome adolescents in school.

Miller's conclusions were reflected in a local Chicago study. Edward Tromanhauser, a professor at Chicago State University, and his colleagues (Tromanhauser et al., 1981), conducted a massive survey of over 12,000 students in Chicago public schools. The report concluded that school-based gang activity could be found in all 20 of Chicago's school districts. Just over half of the students surveyed reported that gangs were active in their schools, and 10 percent reported being either intimidated or attacked by gang members, or solicited for membership.

The minority dropout rate in Chicago schools in the 1980s was one of the largest, if not the largest, in the nation. At least one study blamed the high rates of school dropout by minorities in Chicago schools on the level of gang activity. Ray Hutchison and Father Charles Kyle (1984) published the study. In 1983, Father Kyle (1984) interviewed random samples of the 1979 entering classes of two predominantly Latino/a Chicago high schools. On the basis of these interviews, the researchers concluded that gangs controlled specific classrooms and whole floors at the two schools included in the study. Drugs, including cocaine and heroin, were reported to be routinely sold inside the schools by gang members. Administrators had not attempted to control this situation. Nongang students and students who were members of rival gangs (those not in control in their schools) made a transition from avoiding gang-controlled parts of the schools by cutting classes to ultimately dropping out.

Despite these research efforts, we have come to identify gang control of schools as a greatly exaggerated condition. What led us to this conclusion? First, findings from other available studies of gang members and schools runs counter to the idea that gangs control schools. Second, the studies alleging gang control rely on the reports of school officials and self-reports of nongang member students and dropouts. The studies that we use to challenge these results include these kinds of studies, but also include studies that use official records and interviews with gang members themselves. Finally, a great deal of the research upon which the idea that gangs control schools has been based was conducted in Chicago. A substantial portion of the counterfindings also comes from Chicago studies.

In his classic extended research on Chicago gangs, Thrasher (1927, p. 5) observed that gang problems in schools were less serious in nature than gang problems outside schools. The durability of Thrasher's conclusion was substantiated by a 1980s study of Chicago Public Schools by Irving Spergel (1985). Spergel conducted an analysis of official records data from the Chicago Police Department and Chicago Public Schools. A key finding was that only 9 percent of Chicago's officially recorded gang crime occurred in or near public schools. Spergel concluded, in concurrence with Thrasher, that the school gang problem was distinctly different from the street gang problem. Based on his analysis of official records and his decades of conducting and reviewing research on gangs, Spergel (1995) has described the gang problem as it is manifested in public schools as representing the activity of younger gang members and involving less serious offenses. On the other hand, the gang problem as it is manifested on the streets involves older gang members and more serious offenses.

A number of studies have drawn attention to the major reason for the lower level of gang violence in schools in comparison to surrounding communities: *gang members are not in school.* Felix Padilla (1992) studied a drug-selling Puerto Rican gang in Chicago. The gang that he gave the fictitious name the Diamonds had been a fighting gang before reorganizing itself for drug selling. All of the members of the Diamonds with whom Padilla came in contact had dropped out of school.

A similar finding was offered by John Hagedorn (1988, p. 116) from his study of gang founders in Milwaukee. Hagedorn attributed the rise of Milwaukee gangs to a school bussing policy that closed inner-city schools and forced minority youths to travel to school in more middle-class neighborhoods. Initially the Milwaukee gangs claimed their goal as self-protection against nonminority students in their new schools, but ultimately conflicts between gangs of the same ethnicity became more important as sources of violence. While half of the gang founders interviewed by Hagedorn had parents who had graduated from high school, none of the gang founders themselves had finished high school.

Decker and Van Winkle (1996, pp. 194–95) interviewed active gang members in St. Louis. Some of what gang members told them could selectively be used to support the belief that gangs control schools. For example, one 20-year-old gang member recollected that during his school days, he had carried two pistols to school every day. By his account, he had bribed school security guards with crack cocaine. Others gang members recalled bribing teachers and selling drugs to teachers. Yet, Decker and Van Winkle were emphatic in their conclusions that gangs *did not* run schools or even parts of schools. They labeled accounts of gangs controlling schools as "alarmist and unfounded" (p. 191). They concluded (p. 204), "We would not deny that drug sales, gang fights, and gun carrying are serious problems in the schools our subjects attended. But, these schools are not controlled by omnipotent gangs who hold the student and adult populations in terror."

Decker and Van Winkle reported that one-fifth of the gang members that they interviewed in St. Louis had graduated from high school and two-fifths were still enrolled in high school. However, the in-school behaviors described to the researchers by gang members in school suggested that their finishing school would be unlikely. Truancy and rule-violating behaviors were the most common activities reported when questions about school were asked. If we look at Decker and Van Winkle's (p. 190) gang study population in terms of only those who were no longer in school, the graduation rate for gang members in St. Louis would be one in three or 33.3 percent, considerably less than that of the population as a whole.

In Irving Spergel's (1995) words, "Participant observation and informant studies over three decades consistently indicate that gang members are typically behind in their studies or are school drop-outs." According to Thrasher (1927, p. 341), two factors led to the absence of gang members in schools: (1) the things that are done in school are of little interest to gang members, and (2) schools don't have the resources to intervene effectively with gang members. This second condition leaves the school only one way to respond to gang members—suspending them. These two conditions provide the basis for two alternative ideas about why gang members leave school.

Gangs Pull Members Away From School

Gangs offer their own set of values, opportunities for achievement, and sources of status to youths. Gangs' organization and their structural location in the network of enmities and alliances require varying levels of commitment from their members. As the complexity of gang symbols, rituals, and ideas increase, so does the intellectual energy required for full participation. The greater the level of a youth's commitment to a gang, the lower his or her commitment to the cultural system represented by school participation.

As noted above, most of the St. Louis gang members interviewed by Decker and Van Winkle described their activity in school as engaging in non-school-oriented behavior such as skipping classes and violating rules. Usually these activities were carried out in association with and with the moral support of their gang peers. Most of the gang members reported participating in more school extracurricular activities before becoming involved in their gang than after. The demands of being "down for colors" were too often in clear opposition to school achievement. Decker and Van Winkle attributed many of the violent incidents that erupted at school and that invariably brought gang members into conflict with school authorities as having a basis in street-based gang rivalries.

James Diego Vigil (1988) portrayed gang involvement as commitment to an alternative culture that is distinctly different from the cultural message of the school. Padilla (1992) also described the difficulties that his gang member informants had with school authority as a form of "oppositional or resistance" behavior. Moore (1991) felt that interpreting gang involvement as a resistance that encourages its members to "subvert and defy the norms and ideals of the schools" may be accurate. She cautioned, however, that it is resistance that dooms gang members. It is a form of defiance that she felt assures gang members of failure in school and in work, and at worst can become "an effective socialization for prison."

Gang Members Are Pushed Out of Schools

According to Thrasher (1927), the increased surveillance by adult authority that exists in public schools in comparison to other places in the social world of gang members is enough to keep gang youth away from the schools or in trouble much of the time that they are there. Padilla's (1992) discussion of school attendance by his gang member informants supports this suggestion. Though Padilla's gang members had their share of discipline problems, several reported continuing participation in school in order to sell drugs there. Once a 1986 law placed stiffer penalties on youths selling drugs at school, these gang members stopped attending.

Most of the gang founders whom Hagedorn (1988, p. 116) reported as having dropped out of school had been kicked out for fighting. As Decker and Van Winkle (1996, p. 228) have noted, "Schools do not want students who sell drugs, fight with rivals, show disrespect for teachers and staff, and carry weapons." Reflecting Thrasher's point above, Malcolm Klein (1995) has suggested that it is the school's inability to deal with gang problems in other ways that so often leads to their pursuit of suppression strategies. In particular, it is school administrators' tendency to turn to law enforcement for assistance in dealing with gang problems that leads to their zero tolerance for gang members and, thereby, to gang intervention programs.

As with many of the ideas that we present in this book, the "pull" and "push" propositions of how gang members leave school may both have an element of truth. Future research into gang and school involvement will have to attempt to distinguish between the two types of influences as well as identify interactions between them.

Before we leave the topic of gangs and schools, a curious experiment that occurred in a Chicago school must be noted. Under support from the local community, the school administration of the Englewood Technical Preparatory Academy, a public school, enlisted factions of the Black Gangster Disciple Nation, a Chicago street gang with a recorded history of crime and violence, to bring order to the school. Gang members patrolled the halls and "disciplined" students for not doing their homework or performing well on tests. The four-year experiment finally came to an end in late 1996 with almost all involved, especially parents and school officials, considering the program a mistake and a failure.

The Criminal Justice System

As we enumerate and describe the institutions that affect the lives of gang members, it is particularly telling that the criminal justice system follows our description of families and schools. For a growing number of youths, the criminal justice system plays a more important role in their lives. The United States has increasingly come to rely upon incarceration as a means to solve the crime problem, and as it does so, contacts between gang members and agents of the criminal justice system increase.

The Police

How do the police respond to gangs, and what is the nature of the interaction between gang members and the police? In the next chapter, we will detail the response of the criminal justice system to gangs; however, in this chapter we attempt to capture the nature of gang members' involvement with the police. We can summarize these experiences quite nicely with a single word: extensive. Most field studies of gangs report that almost all gang members have been arrested at some time, and surveys of gang members consistently find that gang members are arrested more often than their nongang peers. Gang members see the police regularly, in large part because gang members spend so much time "hanging out," standing on street corners, in parks, and outside their houses. This makes them visible to the police, and not surprisingly, the police avail themselves of the opportunity to talk with gang members and often to provide curbstone justice, informal adjustments that involve admonishments, advice, and information gathering.

The police response to gangs is generally twofold, to gather information for intelligence purposes and to engage in suppression activities. Depending on the police assignment and activity of the gang members, these interactions can either be hostile and aggressive, spirited exchanges, or nonantagonistic. Many cities have created special gang intelligence units, whose function is to gather information for policy formulation, plan strategic interventions, or tip off other police units about upcoming gang activities. Because arrests are often left to other units in the department, gang members can develop rapport with these officers and often report having positive relationships with such officers. However, most gang members, not surprisingly, report antagonistic relationships with police officers, and a generalized distrust of the criminal justice system. This is a matter of concern, since the first agent of government most citizens interact with is typically a law enforcement officer, and perceptions of that interaction are generalized to other government agencies.

Prisons and Gangs

There is growing evidence that prison propels many young men toward gang membership who formerly were not gang members. Imprisonment strengthens the ties between many gang members and their gangs, as gang affiliation is one of the few remaining sources of identification open to incarcerated gang members. In many states, there is growing concern about the influence of gangs in prisons.

Prison plays an increasingly important role in the lives of gang members, for two reasons. First, as gang members become more involved in crime, their likelihood of being arrested, convicted, and going to prison increases substantially. Thus, prison is a natural extension of gang life, and gangs can play an important role in prison by regulating the lives of members. But there is a second reason why prisons are increasingly important to gang members. Many of the older gang members who go to prison were leaders in their gangs, and the gangs they leave behind often continue to depend on them for their leadership. Thus gang members on the street may find that imprisoned gang members are calling the "shots"—where to sell drugs, whom to target for violence, and what new coalitions to form—for gang members on the street. The leader of the largest street gang in Chicago, Larry Hoover of the Gangster Disciples, is reputed to have run his gang for years, and some claim more effectively, while incarcerated in the Illinois prison system.

Going to prison can also provide gang members with additional status. In some Los Angeles and Chicago gangs, members report that unless individuals have gone to prison, they cannot assume a position of leadership in the gang. Thus a continuum from the street to prison and back to the street is formed as the prison becomes yet one more step in the rites of passage that comprise gang life. In more organized gangs, there are reports that the families of imprisoned members are taken care of, and often money is forwarded to imprisoned members for use in the prison. Moore (1988) reported that this is especially true of the Mexican-American gang members she studied in southern California, many of whom were recruited while in prison and find a familiar community of associates upon their release as a consequence of prison gang involvement.

It is important to distinguish between prison and street gangs. While there are relationships between the two, it is not a seamless move from one to the another, and the differences can be quite profound. Because men and women in prison are older and more involved in crime than gang members on the street, prison gangs are more organized and more disciplined than their counterparts on the street. Indeed, prison gangs can be quite ruthless in enforcing discipline, and since prison life affords little room for secrecy or privacy, most aspects of an individual's life are well-known to fellow inmates.

Politics

The link between gangs and politics has a substantial historical legacy. In his account of early 20th-century Chicago gangs, Frederic Thrasher (1927, pp. 313–36) devoted an entire chapter to gang involvement in politics. Irving Spergel (1995, p. 120) has suggested that youth gangs can serve as "a source of stability and potential power" for local politicians. In particular, he described the working relationships between ward bosses and their local gangs. The nature of the involvement between gangs and politics has varied with the structure of local politics. Gangs were integrally involved in the operations of the Tweed machine in New York City in the 1800s (Spergel, 1995, p. 120). In Philadelphia during that century, volunteer fire companies were central to local politics. These fire companies frequently drew their membership from local youth gangs. Bursik and Grasmick (1993) provided an account of how the alliance between the youth gang the Hamburgs and politicians in the Bridgeport neighborhood of Chicago in the early decades of the 20th century laid a political foundation for that community's later control of the office of the city's mayor.

During the riots in the late 1960s Chicago, Spergel (1995, p. 121) identified evidence that gang members were enlisted by the Chicago police to assist them in quelling the social disorder. Even more recently gangs were very involved in the 1986 primary elections in a predominantly Puerto Rican ward of Chicago (p. 122.) Rival gangs supported different candidates, and one of the candidates even made a former gang leader coordinator of his precinct captains.

There are a number of ways these relationships between gangs and politicians have proved mutually useful to both. From the politician's perspective, Thrasher (1927, p. 313) noted, "The political boss finds gangs, whether composed of boys or of men above voting age, very useful in promoting the interests of his machine." Thrasher further suggested that many of the Chicago political bosses knew exactly how to appeal to gang members because they themselves were graduates of the street gangs. Bursik and Grasmick (1993, p. 177) reminded us that the most famous former member of the Bridgeport youth gang the Hamburgs was the late Mayor Richard J. Daley, Sr. Thrasher provided a list of the ways in which street gang members assist politicians. The list included the distribution of campaign literature, the posting of signs, and assisting voters to get to the polls. Most of these tasks are those assigned to any campaign workers, but gangs have been reported to have gone beyond these kinds of tasks. Kornblum (1974, p. 166) reported that in Chicago politics gangs were also relied on for "the systematic removal of the opposition's street signs and lamp posters." From his study of gangs in three cities, Martin Sanchez-Jankowski (1991, p. 216) stated, "All thirty-seven gangs observed throughout the ten years of this study established some type of *expedient-exchange* relationship with the politicians in their city." In addition to those services provided by gangs to politicians listed by Thrasher, Sanchez-Jankowski's (pp.

219-220) list included intimidation through physical presence at the polls on election day and occasionally harassment of campaign critics and opposition workers.

Suggesting the durability of the pattern of gang-politician relationships over time, Sanchez-Jankowski's (pp. 220-25) list of what gangs receive from politicians was identical to that of Thrasher. These benefits included resources, influence, and protection. Resources provided to gang members by politician allies have ranged from direct payment to provision of office space and city support in obtaining external funding. The post-election influence of gang members has had its most extreme manifestation in the appointment of gang members to staff positions. Finally, protection, the most sinister of the benefits, took the form in Thrasher's time of collaboration, bootlegging, and nonenforcement of bootlegging laws. Sanchez-Jankowski described similar more contemporary "understandings" between city officials and law enforcement agencies with respect to gang drug-trafficking operations.

As with much gang behavior, reported involvement between gangs and politicians has varied across locales. Spergel (1995, p. 120) has hypothesized that such relationships are more likely "in times of rapid change and social turmoil." While Sanchez-Jankowski noted that all of the gangs that he studied had some relationships with public officials, he reported that only in New York and Boston did gangs have "consistent and direct contact with the offices of elected mayoral and council politicians." For none of the gangs that he studied in Los Angeles did he observe such stable relationships with elected officials. Perhaps another factor is the stability of the gang situation. Most of the examples described above have been taken from chronic gang problem cities. Viable involvement in politics by gang members was described by neither Hagedorn in Milwaukee nor Decker and Van Winkle in St. Louis. Both of these sites were jurisdictions with emerging gang problems.

Involvement of gangs in politics has the potential for a great deal of social harm. For Thrasher (1927, p. 320) relationships between gangs and politicians facilitate more extensive alliances between crime and politics and ultimately lead to government corruption. Spergel (1995, p. 121) has concluded that gangs are not "ordinarily" committed to social and political causes. When gangs were called upon to quell social disorders in Chicago, Spergel (1995, p. 121) noted that gang members protected some local merchant property during riots only for a fee.

Particularly noteworthy have been efforts by Chicago street gangs to expand their political influence. During the 1970s, the Vice Lords obtained hundreds of thousands of dollars in external grants from government agencies and private foundations (Jacobs, 1978; Dawley, 1973, 1992). The El Rukns have attempted a wide variety of political involvement. The El Rukns were formerly known as the Blackstone Rangers and later as the P Stone Rangers. In all of these organizational incarnations, the gang engaged in levels of political organizing from the 1960s to the 1980s (Sale 1972; Toobin 1994). They have supported local candidates and formed voter mobilization groups. On the other hand, the leader of the El Rukns, Jeff Forte, was indicted for conspiring to solicit Libyan funding in exchange for engaging in domestic terrorism (Toobin, 1994). The 1990s have been marked by a foray into political legitimacy by the Black Gangster Disciple Nation (BGDN). The group's letters were argued to stand for Black Growth and Development Network. Twenty-first Century Voices of Total Empowerment (VOTE), a community-based group, spawned by BGDN leadership gained the support of Jesse Jackson's Operation Push, of James Compton of the Urban League, a former mayor of Chicago, and of at least two members of the city council in its voter registration drives. When federal authorities indicted 39 GBDN leaders in August 1995, leaders of VOTE and candidates for office were included in the indictment along with incarcerated gang leaders.

Labor Market

The two major institutions in a child's life are the family and the school. Above we noted sociologist William Julius Wilson's concerns about the future of these institutions in the inner-city communities where gang problems are greatest. From Wilson's (1985, 1996) perspective, the threats to the stability and effectiveness of families and schools have their roots in the changing U.S. economy. In the last two decades, the United States has experienced a dramatic economic restructuring. Manufacturing jobs have been greatly diminished in number as a result of automation and companies relocating to rural areas or other countries. For inner-city residents, available industrial jobs have all but vanished. The service economy that has grown with the decline in manufacturing is characterized by less stable and lower-paying jobs. For Wilson, work is the fundamental element of the community. As work disappears, families become unstable and the connection between school and getting a job ceases to exist. Without stable and effective families and schools, the interpersonal relationships, community businesses, and political structures that give communities strength also disappear (Bursik and Grasmick, 1993, p. 177).

Joan Moore (1988) and John Hagedorn (1988) were the first to assert that the growth of the urban underclass as formulated by Wilson was having a profound effect on the nation's gang problems. The primary piece of evidence linking gangs to the growth of the underclass for Moore and Hagedorn was the extension of gang involvement into adulthood. Back when Thrasher (1927) studied gangs, he described gang activity as a transitional phenomenon that ended as the adolescent gang member became an adult. Research in the 1960s such as that of Irving Spergel (1964) and Malcolm Klein (1971) observed the same condition. Gang involvement ended as gang members took on the responsibilities of marriage and employment. Observing Mexican American gang members in Los Angeles and African American gang members in Milwaukee continue their gang involvement into adulthood, Moore and Hagedorn hypothesized that this continued involvement had to be a function of the absence of viable employment for these young men and women. Especially in Milwaukee, where Hagedorn had conducted his research, the emergence of gangs and de-industrialization could be clearly paralleled. Pamela Irving Jackson (1991) suggested a fundamental link between inner-city crime, gangs, and the social dislocations associated with national-level economic transitions. Decker and Van Winkle observed just that kind of pattern in the emergence of St. Louis gangs and shifts in the city's labor market. Malcolm Klein (1995, p. 194) has joined these researchers in listing the emerging urban underclass as the primary cause of the proliferation of gang problem cities across the nation.

At the time of his study, three-quarters of Hagedorn's gang founders were still involved in their gangs. Hagedorn (1988, pp. 124-25) determined that among his gang founders only 10 percent were employed full-time. Of those employed, no one was reported as making more than $5 per hour. Still, Hagedorn (1994) found that since becoming adults, most former gang members had worked more months in legitimate low-paying jobs than they had spent selling drugs or engaging in other illegal activity. Moore (1991, pp. 115-16) noted that among the former Mexican American gang members whom she interviewed in Los Angeles, "work was the primary survival strategy," just not one in which they were especially successful. About 40 percent of the former gang members she studied were unemployed with variations associated with age and gender. Many had evidence of trying to maintain jobs. Almost all (85 percent) had worked at some time over the preceding five years. Moore listed the alternative survival strategies to work as being supported by family, government transfers such as welfare, and illegal activity. Less than a fifth of the St. Louis gang members interviewed by Decker and Van Winkle were employed in the legitimate labor market. Decker and Van Winkle(1994, 1996; Decker 1996) suggested unemployment among gang members was a dual result of the unavailability of viable jobs and the unemployable skills of gang members. From communities ravaged by unemployment, gang members lacked the social connections and personal control required for getting and keeping a job.

A more cynical picture of gang members' attitudes toward work is offered by Sanchez-Jankowski (1991, p. 240). He described gang members as working to "avoid" the low-paying service jobs that were available. Most job programs for gang members, Sanchez-Jankowski asserted, provided access only to those kinds of jobs. When gang members participated in such programs, their primary goal was temporary spending money rather than legitimate work. When the gang members that he interviewed did obtain legitimate work, the modest pay and routine led them to quit in order to return to their pursuit of "large amounts of capital" through "illegal business ventures."

For the gang members studied by Felix Padilla (1992, p. 16) in Chicago, there was in their minds a direct relationship between the gang and "making money." The gang was, in other words, for many members a form of work. Mitchell Duneier (1992, p. 39) studied the regular customers at a cafeteria not far from the University of Chicago. He noted among the patrons a passion for respectability and order. For those patrons without the stability of a full-time job, this respectability was pursued by arranging their lives in recurring patterns of behavior. Being at the same place and doing the same things with the same people at the same times each day was highly valued by the men observed by Duneier. Perhaps, for younger men faced with the same needs for respectability and order and a similar inability to achieve them through employment, the gang plays an important part in providing both.

Summary

Gang members interact with a variety of social institutions such as schools, the labor market, and the criminal justice system. In this regard, they are much like their nongang counterparts. However, the quality and frequency of interactions with institutions like the school or a job are much weaker and more infrequent. Gang members have increased contact with law enforcement. The configuration of institutional contacts serves to pull the gang closer together.

Chapter Seven

Responding to Gang-Related Crime and Delinquency

When he was 8 years old, Jared's 14-year-old brother was killed in a gang-related shooting. By default, Jared considered himself a member of his brother's gang, and members of his brother's and rival gangs made the same assumption. Within a few months of his brother's death, Jared received his first referral to the juvenile court for vandalism. Before his 10th birthday, he was referred to the court a total of four times, for disturbing the peace, for trespassing, and twice for petty theft. Finally, when he was 10, Jared stole a pistol from another boy. Before the day was over, he had used the pistol to wound an older youth in what he felt was self-defense. After a stay in a residential juvenile facility, Jared was selected for aftercare in a special program for serious, chronic, and violent offenders. He was delivered to his new case manager in shackles and handcuffs. The experienced probation officer needed to have a good deal of paper work completed with Jared's assistance. She attempted to make a game of the processing. She offered to remove his handcuffs after half of the paperwork was finished. The shackles would come off when all of the paperwork was finished. The case officer and Jared finished half of the paperwork. The case officer removed the handcuffs and placed them on her desk. While they were working on the second half of the paperwork, the case officer was distracted by a question from another probation officer. When she returned to working with Jared, she noticed that the handcuffs were missing from her desk. It did not take too long to realize that Jared had stolen the handcuffs and hidden them in his clothing. After six months in a variety of social service programs, the case officer and other profes-

sionals who were working with Jared continued to worry about the po-
tential for the youngster to begin functioning as an ordinary 12-year-old.

A s Walter Miller (1982, p. 147) noted over 10 years ago, we
have spent "over half a century" responding to gang-related
crime with programs and policies. In this chapter, we review what
we have learned from over five decades of responding to gang-related crime. In addition to reviewing what we know, we examine
some of the gaps that exist in the literature about gangs and make
recommendations about what issues need to be discussed in developing future responses to gang-related crime and delinquency.

Categories of Response Strategies

In this section, we identify response categories and briefly describe the effect of prominent programs under each category, con-
centrating on programs that have been evaluated. We focus on programs that were specifically designed to respond to gang-related
crime rather than to general or non-gang-related crime and delinquency problems.

In 1988, Irving Spergel and David Curry (1990, 1993) surveyed
254 agency representatives from 45 cities and 6 institutional sites as
part of the Office of Juvenile Justice and Delinquency Prevention
(OJJDP) National Youth Gang Suppression and Intervention Program (NYGSIP). Respondents answered open-ended questions on
program activities, priority of strategies employed, and estimates
of effectiveness of agency efforts. From their analysis of respondent
answers, the researchers constructed five categories of response
strategies, shown in Figure 7-1. Spergel (1995, p. 171) suggested that
four of the strategies—community organization, social intervention,
opportunities provision, and suppression—"have assumed some
dominance in a particular historical period."

The goal of the NYGSIP survey was to identify promising programs that existed in 1988. Detailed descriptions of the most promising of those programs from five communities and one correctional
site can be found in Spergel and Chance (1990). Those promising
projects studied by Spergel and his colleagues from 1988 to 1991
were used to develop prototypes and models for new programs
(Spergel et al., 1992a, 1992b). Five community-level programs based
on these models were implemented in 1995 with the support of

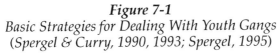

Figure 7-1
Basic Strategies for Dealing With Youth Gangs
(*Spergel & Curry, 1990, 1993; Spergel, 1995*)

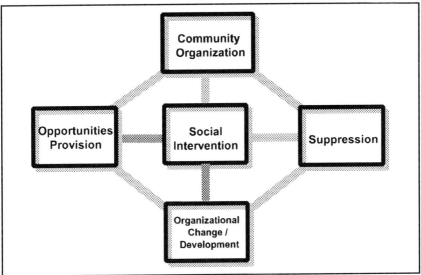

OJJDP's Comprehensive Response to America's Gang Problem
(OJJDP, 1994).

Only a few recent programs are described here due to a gap of more than a decade in which the criminal justice system and many researchers "forgot" or avoided the subject of gang problems (Bookin-Weiner and Horowitz, 1983; Miller, 1990). If we want to learn from gang response programs that have been systematically evaluated, we have to study programs conducted and studied prior to 1980, or we will have to wait for the completed evaluations of programs that have begun since our nation's rediscovery of gang problems in the late 1980s.

Community Organization

When Spergel (1964, p. 183) outlined community action responses to delinquency problems in the final chapter of his study of New York City gangs, he included "organization" as one of three major categories. In a subsequent work, Spergel (1969, p. 20) used the term *interorganizing* to describe "efforts at enhancing, modification, or change in intergroup or interorganizational relationships to cope with a community problem." Spergel and Curry (1993, pp. 371–72) classified all strategies that attempted to create community solidarity, education, and involvement as forms of "community organization." "Networking" was considered the most basic community organization strategy so long as it was not restricted to justice system agencies. Multiple agency prevention efforts and advocacy for victims were also included in this strategic area.

Frederic Thrasher's (1927) research on Chicago gangs in the early decades of this century incorporated a community organization approach. Thrasher's plan for responding to gang crime problems had six components, as shown in Table 7-1. Thrasher felt that authority for the community response had to be concentrated in one agency that could be held directly accountable to community residents. To be effective, local programs had to be based on timely and systematic social research. Services intended to prevent gang involvement had to be "integrated," whether such services were targeted at an individual child, a family, or a gang. By being aimed at all children in an at-risk area, programs insured inclusion of the most delinquent youths whom Thrasher assumed were the most likely not to be involved in programs. Throughout his ideal response process, Thrasher maintained that an effective response required community residents to be continuously informed and educated. Thrasher's ideas were never implemented or subjected to evaluation, but, with added influence from Clifford Shaw and Henry McKay (1943), these ideas are reflected in the best-known community organization responses to gang crime problems of this cen-

Table 7-1
Components of Thrasher's Community "Reorganization" Strategy
(Thrasher, 1927, p. 364)

Concentrate Responsibility
Base Program on Social Research
Integrate Services
Apply Program *Systematically* to All *Children*
Create New Agencies
Inform & Educate the Public

tury—the Chicago Area Project (1929–62), New York City's Mobilization for Youth (1961–67), and Philadelphia's Crisis Intervention Network (1974–87).

The Chicago Area Project. The Chicago Area Project (CAP) was developed to designate program target sectors that were labeled "delinquency areas" by Shaw and McKay (1972; Roberts, 1989). From these community assessments, the goals of the Chicago Area Project were to develop local community organizations to fill gaps in social control and to develop indigenous leadership and neighborhood organization (Klein, 1971, p. 44). The guiding theory was Shaw and McKay's concept of "social disorganization," an approach to understanding delinquency that examines the social ecology of neighborhoods. Six neighborhood committees were formed in selected Chicago delinquency areas. Each committee was empowered to choose its own director and to make decisions about responding to delinquency in its community. The staff of CAP served as community organizers and consultants for these neighborhood committees and assisted the committees in obtaining the resources needed to develop the responses and programs that the committee selected. CAP staff assisted the committees in establishing regular communication and interaction with criminal justice, school, and social agency representatives. Assisting individual at-risk youths to complete educational goals and obtain employment were primary activities of the committees. Formal and informal networks of community individuals and groups strengthened and supplemented by CAP efforts were the major program activity. Steven Schlossman and Maurice Sedlak (1983, pp. 449–62) offer in their history of the long-running CAP an overview of systematic and nonsystematic evaluations. One of the best known critiques of CAP is found in Saul Alinsky's *Reveille for Radicals* (1946). As a young CAP street worker, Alinsky decided that his assigned neighborhood committee was inadequate for the "real" needs of community residents and developed his more confrontational approach as an alternative kind of community response. In 1944, Clifford Shaw, who served as director and lead researcher of CAP, produced a statistical study that showed reductions in delinquency rates in at least one CAP target community. Schlossman and Sedlak (pp. 456–57) noted that resultant criticism of his statistical methods and his interpretations of the social processes of community life led Shaw to shy away from subsequent efforts to support the success of CAP with conventional social science methodology. Schlossman and Sedlak (p. 459) concluded that in terms of implementation the program must be regarded as a success. In terms of reducing delinquency, measurement issues (not unknown in today's efforts to evaluate programs) make impact evaluation conclusions impossible.

Mobilization for Youth, New York City. The goals of the Mobilization for Youth (MFY) (1961–67) were to restructure the social organization of the Lower East Side of Manhattan through community participation and special programs to involve residents in expanded opportunities. Originally funded by the National Institute of Mental Health, in 1962 the MFY was the recipient of an action grant from the President's Committee on Juvenile Delinquency and Youth Crime. Richard Cloward was the theoretical progenitor and briefly research director of MFY. Just as Shaw's "social disorganization" theory defined CAP, Cloward and Ohlin's (1960) "opportunity theory" shaped MFY. Opportunities provision and community service were primary goals in the context of community organization and the creation of "indigenous" institutions. At the heart of the institution-building process was the Lower East Side Association. The project was central to the War on Poverty and Great Society strategies of President Johnson's administration. A youth service corps was established, first hiring unemployed youths and using many of them to teach younger children to read. Special programs focused on gang-involved youths, but delinquency prevention programs targeted all children in the community (Bibb, 1967). From community organizations that focused on mobilizing local resources, MFY grew into a social action movement challenging New York City and the powers that be in confrontational strategies similar to those that Alinsky had advocated for CAP (Bursik and Grasmick, 1993, p. 168). Malcolm Klein (1971, p. 44) reported that no specific evaluations of MFY programs were known to him. As with CAP, there is sufficient evidence (Bibb, 1967; Kahn, 1967; Bursik and Grasmick, 1993) that MFY was a success in terms of process evaluation outcomes in the development of the desired community organizations. There was no systematic evaluation of its impact on delinquency or gang involvement.

Crisis Intervention Network, Philadelphia. Philadelphia's Crisis Intervention Network (CIN) (1974–87) was primarily a community organization approach, but like CAP and MFY, CIN had components that reflected other strategic approaches and coexisted with a grassroots community organization, House of Umoja. With a street work and probation/parole unit, CIN represented a coalition of neighborhood-level community organizations. According to Spergel (1995, p. 253), CIN was "a suppression or surveillance strategy ... added to a social intervention or youth outreach approach within a community mobilization framework in which all key elements of the community, legitimate and illegitimate, joined to reduce the level of gang crime." The House of Umoja was an independent "shelter for at-risk youths" with an emphasis on building self-respect through an awareness of African American culture and traditions. The House of Umoja pioneered the utilization of gang summits and truces to reduce street violence. The CIN umbrella also extended to parents' groups and other grassroots organizations. There is no systematic process evaluation of the CIN project, and it was not based on any particular theory of gangs or delinquency. CIN remains worthy of attention due to the decline in gang-related homicides for Philadelphia in the 1970s—43 in 1973, 32 in 1974, six in 1975, and one in 1977 (Needle and Stapleton, 1983). In 1992, the Philadelphia Police Department reported that it did not maintain records on gang-related homicides and in 1994 did not officially recognize the presence of a gang crime problem. Without systematic evaluations, it is impossible to know what role gang response programs played in the perceived decline of Philadelphia's gang problem.

Social Intervention

Social intervention encompasses both social service agency-based programs and what are generally referred to as "street work" or "detached worker" programs. According to Spergel (1966, p. 27), street work is

> the practice variously labeled detached work, street club, gang work, area work, extension youth work, corner work, etc. It is the systematic effort of an agency worker, through social work or treatment techniques within the neighborhood context, to help a group of young people who are described as delinquent or partially delinquent to achieve a conventional adaptation. It involves the redirection or conversion of youth gangs to legitimate social gangs or conventional organizations. This requires the agent to work

with or manipulate the people or other agency representatives who interact critically with members of the delinquent group.

For Klein (1971, p. 44), among social service approaches, only the detached worker program "has been identified as a 'pure' gang approach." The rationale for this assumption is that gang members either fail to make use of or are barred from other youth services and engage in self-destructive, antisocial behavior that necessitates an outreach action to interrupt the cycle. As Spergel (1995, p. 174) noted, an assumption of this approach was that "the juvenile gang had positive potential; only selected negative structural and process elements required modification. . . . The gang itself was to be a vehicle of its own transformation." As noted above, community mobilization approaches have often contained social intervention components. Next we look at descriptions of selected landmark detached worker programs.

Midcity Project, Boston. The Boston Midcity Project (1954–57) was a street work project that was conducted in conjunction with community mobilization components. According to Walter Miller (1962, p. 169), the project was "directed at three societal units seen to figure importantly in the genesis and perpetuation of delinquent behavior—the community, the family, and the gang." Work with gangs was, however, the major effort of the project. Seven project detached workers were assigned to "an area, group, or groups with a mandate to contact, establish relationships with, and attempt to change resident gangs." Each worker was professionally trained and had access to psychiatric consultation "so that workers were in a position to utilize methods and perspectives of psychodynamic psychiatry in addition to the group dynamics and recreational approaches in which they had been trained." The target gangs included African American and white gangs and male and female groups. The program demonstrated that it was possible for professionally trained adults to establish contact and interact closely with gang members over a period of time. For Miller, the principal impact evaluation question was, "Was there a significant measurable inhibition of law-violating or morally disapproved behavior as a consequence of Project efforts?" Miller used three measures of behavior and a control group design to answer his question. He concluded that "no," there was no observable program impact.

Chicago Youth Development Project. The Chicago Youth Development Project (CYDP) 1960–65 was a joint effort by the Chicago Boys Clubs and the Institute for Social Research of the University of Michigan supported by the Ford Foundation (Mattick and Caplan, 1967, p. 107). Though detached street work coordinated by the Boys Clubs was the major focus of the project, a supplementary community organization component was also included. The program included gang and nongang youths, and the research component involved continued feedback to field workers throughout the course of the project program (Caplan et al., 1967). The evaluation report (Gold and Mattick, 1974, cited in Spergel, 1995, p. 249) showed no impact on delinquency. In fact, youths who reported being closest to their program workers showed the greatest levels of delinquency. A subgroup of participants showed an enhancement of educational aspirations, but overall the impact evaluation results did not suggest that the kind of "aggressive street work" employed had an impact on reducing delinquency.

The Group Guidance Project and the Ladino Hills Project, Los Angeles. The Group Guidance Project (GGP) (1961–65) followed the general design of the projects described in Boston and Chicago, while Malcolm Klein anchored the Ladino Hills Program (LHP) (1966–67) around the issue of group cohesion. In the GGP, the detached street workers who worked out of the Los Angeles County Probation Department took their services to four gangs of about 800 total members. The primary goals of the street workers were the control and prevention of gang violence. The results of the evaluation, however, brought Klein to the unsettling conclusion that GGP itself may have increased delinquency among gang members. Specifically, he found that delinquency increased among gang members who received the most services. Cohesion among gang members increased in direct proportion to the attention paid to the gang by street workers, and delinquency increased in conjunction with cohesiveness. These findings led Klein to the conclusion that detached street worker programs do not work, and enhance gang solidarity and promote more violence. LHP gave Klein an opportunity to test his conclusions from GGP. In LHP, Klein took a detached work program with group programming for a Mexican American gang cluster of about 140 members and incrementally decreased group programming services while increasing the access to individual nongang alternative services and activities. As a result, he observed decreases in his measures of cohesion and in the size of the gang. While the number of offenses for active gang members did not decline, overall offenses for gang members declined by 35 percent due to reduction in the size of the gang.

Irving Spergel (1995, p. 175) recognized the re-emergence of social intervention strategies in the late 1980s but in new forms focused primarily on prevention of gang involvement by younger children and crisis intervention. From their 1988 data, Spergel and Curry (1993, p. 372) found that social intervention approaches were the most commonly reported among their respondents, second only to suppression strategies.

Opportunities Provision

Two major theoretical perspectives of the 1950s and 1960s were strain theory and differential opportunity theory. Both underscore the importance of access to legitimate means and opportunities for preventing gang involvement. Under strain theory, youths adopt universal cultural goals that emphasize material success. When the conventional means to achieve culturally mandated goals are not socially available, youth "innovate" and pursue illegitimate means to achieve material success. In differential opportunity theory, Richard Cloward and Lloyd Ohlin (1960) extended strain theory by emphasizing the differential availability of legitimate and illegitimate opportunities to youths. Opportunities provision approaches attempt to offer youths at risk legitimate opportunities and means to success that are at least as appealing as available illegitimate options.

Opportunities strategies are among the most expensive and challenging. Approaches such as job preparation, training, and placement programs, as well as enhancing educational opportunities for gang youths that might enhance careers, are included under this heading. Among their national agency survey respondents, Spergel and Curry (1993 p. 372) found that opportunities strategies were the least likely to be reported as a primary strategy and the least likely strategy to be reported overall. Gang members did benefit from this strategy in the 1960s. It is important to call attention to one program that sought to incorporate gang structure into the process of opportunities provision. In 1967, the U.S. Office of Economic Opportunity funded two job training and job referral centers through Chicago's Woodlawn Organization that were actually staffed and operated, respectively, by the Gangster Disciples and the Blackstone Rangers. A congressional investigation ultimately led to fraud charges against at least one gang leader. Spergel (1972), who conducted the evaluation, found that gang violence increased over the one-year period of the project. Rossi et al. (1980) and Hackler and Hagan (1975) provide reviews of systematically evaluated economic and educational opportunities provision programs, but none of the programs reviewed focus on—or even mention—any particular problems that may be associated with opportunities provision programs for gang-involved youths. Clearly, this is an important issue in considering this strategy.

Suppression

The rise of suppression as the dominant response to gang crime problems in the late 1970s and the 1980s may be a function of growing political conservatism or it may represent a reaction to increased levels of gang violence. Under the category of suppression, Spergel and Curry (1993, p. 374) included arrest, special prosecution, incarceration, intensive supervision, gang intelligence, and networking among criminal justice agencies to the exclusion of nonjustice agencies. The strategy of suppression was the most common response to gang problems reported by respondents to the 1988 OJJDP national survey (p. 372).

The most frequent suppression programs are police department gang crime units, often modeled after the Los Angeles Police Department's CRASH (Community Resources Against Street Hoodlums) program. A 1992 National Institute of Justice (NIJ) survey (Curry et al., 1992) of the police departments in the largest 79 U.S. cities reported specialized police gang units in 53 of them, and the majority were created since 1986. Spergel (1995, p. 177) comments, "The strategy of increased and targeted suppression has not, by itself, been adequate to reduce the gang problem and return 'control of the streets'—the goal of law enforcement agencies—to local citizens." In most cities, no law enforcement agency relies on suppression strategies alone in responding to gang crime problems. Perhaps most important in the current context is the absence of systematic evaluations of suppression programs.

Organizational Development and Change

Organizational development and change are not primary strategies but accompany other approaches to dealing with gangs. These approaches include all efforts at institutional and policy adaptation and development including gang legislation and expanding available resources. Under this perspective, establishing a gang unit can be viewed as an organizational development strategy that elaborates a suppression strategy. In Thrasher's response model (see Table 7-1), four of the six components can be viewed as organizational development strategies designed to produce a community organization strategy.

Gang legislation constitutes a unique kind of organizational development and change response to gang-related crime. Many law enforcement agencies engage in efforts to initiate or modify legislation related to gangs or the gang problem or try to influence legislation pertaining to gangs. Perhaps the best-known gang legislation and one that has served as a model for other jurisdictions was California's 1988 STEP (Street Terrorism Enforcement and Prevention) Act (California Penal Code Section 182.22). STEP creates civil penalties against gang members. Under STEP legislation, the police can obtain a civil injunction against named gang members that prohibits those gang members from congregating in public, carrying beepers, and drinking in public. The civil authority granted by STEP legislation allows the police to circumvent many of the procedural demands of the criminal law. In their review of gang legislation in California over a 10-year period, Pat Jackson and Cary Rudman (1993) argue that most gang legislation, including STEP, represented a form of "moral panic" that was "overwhelmingly devoted to gang suppression" and influenced by law enforcement.

By 1993, 14 of the 50 states had enacted statutes specifically directed at criminal gang activity. According to a study completed by the Institute for Law and Justice (1993) gang legislation can be grouped into two major categories: (1) those providing criminal sanctions for the justice system against offenders in gang-related crimes, and (2) those providing civil remedies for the victims of gang crime. Criminal sanction legislation most often enhanced sentences for those found guilty of committing a gang-related crime or made provisions for segregating incarcerated gang members. Civil remedy approaches have most often attempted to empower citizens to file civil suits against gang members collectively or individually. A major impediment to the effectiveness of gang legislation are court rulings that several specific legislative acts violate the first amendment rights of gang members.

Perceived Effectiveness of Response Strategies

Since most programs lack direct measures of effectiveness, it is important to know if agencies perceive their programs as successful. Spergel and Curry (1993, p. 379) developed measures of perceived program effectiveness. These measures were constructed from three items that were asked of each of 254 agency representatives participating in the survey. Spergel and Curry reported significantly higher levels of perceived effectiveness for community programs where community organization and opportunity provision were primary response strategies.

Continuing Issues in Responding to Gangs

Delinquency Programs or Gang Programs?

A continuing debate is whether specific gang-oriented responses are required for effectively dealing with gang-related crime and delinquency problems. Complicating this issue is the tendency among many researchers, practitioners, and policy makers to make no clear distinction between gang-related delinquency and delinquency that is not gang-related. Having special programs to prevent or intervene in gang involvement is supported by the conclusion that gang membership facilitates delinquency and that gang members commit significantly more offenses than comparable nongang offenders. Faced with reduced funds for youth programs, community representatives often feel that they have to make choices about which youths are to receive program services when program resources are in short supply. Writing off gang-involved youths as "delinquent" beyond the scope of general youth programs can be one result. Tailoring programs funded as gang response programs to focus on nongang youth populations may also occur. One solution to this dilemma would be to follow Thrasher's (1927, p. 364) recommendation that effective gang response programs must encompass the special needs of gang-involved youths, but must also be open to all youths in gang communities.

National Versus Local Responses

Gang response policy is closely tied to community politics. Of the response categories described above, community organization and organizational development strategies most clearly have political implications. Two local political issues—denial and definition—are particularly linked to policy and response. Both the decision to recognize a gang crime problem and how broadly to define the nature of the problem are community-level political decisions that frame the process of response.

Denial. It is perhaps trite to note that it is impossible to develop a response to gang crime problems in a setting where gang problems are not acknowledged to exist. It is also important to emphasize that a "gang response"when gangs do not constitute a problem is what is labeled a "moral panic" (Hagedorn, 1988; Jackson, 1993; Moore, 1991, 1993). Ronald Huff (1989, p. 530) described an "official denial" stage in three of Ohio's largest cities in the mid-1980s. The emergence of Columbus, Ohio, from its denial stage was accelerated by a publicly visible gang-related murder and separate gang-related attacks on the governor's daughter and the mayor's son. Huff argued that official denial "appears to facilitate victimization by gangs, especially in the public schools."

From his research on gangs in Milwaukee, John Hagedorn (1988, pp. 151–58) described the role that denial can play in shaping the course of a community's response to its gang problem. According to Hagedorn, the motivations for Milwaukee's policy of denial grew out of two kinds of fear. On one hand, political and business leaders of the community feared that recognition of a gang problem would undermine tourism and potential for attracting prospective employers and economic ventures. On the other hand, some segments of the community feared that law enforcement would use "gang problems" as an excuse to "crack down" on poor and minority communities and that any recognition of a gang problem constituted a form of racism. Ultimately, Hagedorn suggested that the real problem with denial is that once gangs are recognized, the initial response to gang-related crime is too often repression because, by the time recognition occurs, community division is so great that the problem will have reached extreme levels. A community strategy that is overly centered on suppression strategies can result, in Hagedorn's view, in minority communities not getting access to resources needed to deal with the social problems that are the root causes of the gang problem in the first place.

In Table 7-2, we contrast researcher and practitioner models of gang problem responses. In contrast to the researcher's view, the practitioner model assumed a link between levels of gang violence and each level of law enforcement response. The models appear to be comparable and each requires an alternative strategic outcome that breaks the cycle of denial and repression. Table 7-2 places the two models side by side and suggests comparable ideal outcome response stages for each. Each response stage is linked to a "reaction paradigm" from criminological theory. The final stage is linked to a paradigm that incorporates the appeal and logic of the separate paradigms of value conflict and social disorganization that have been frequently associated with the emergence and development of gang problems and is compatible with community-level research-based responses to gang crime problems (Spergel, 1995).

Definitional Issues. From a survey of members of a politically appointed gang task force, members of a police gang unit, and a population of juvenile detainees, Decker and Leonard (1991) uncovered a divergence in perspective on the magnitude and nature of

Table 7-2
*Proposed Model of Criminal Justice Reaction to Gang Violence
(Curry, Ball, & Fox, 1994b)*

Hagedorn's Stages Hagedorn (1988)	Curtsinger's Phases NIJ (1992)	Dominant Reaction Paradigm
Denial	Ambiguous Signs/ Criminal Justice Disregards	Social Pathology
	Clear Signs/Informal Denial	Labeling Theory
	Gang-Related Violence/ Official Denial	
Recognition	Increased Violence/Reassessment	Value Conflict
	Dramatic Event/ "Scrambling"	Social Disorganization
	External Pressure/Loss of Focus	
Repression	Institutionalized Gang Problem/ Preoccupation	Critical Perspective
Effectively Organized Response	Multiple Strategies Based on Perceived Causes	Systemic Control

the gang crime problem in St. Louis. Establishing uniformity in gang definitions across jurisdictions is important to researchers and law enforcement officials alike. A major recommendation of the Office of Juvenile Justice and Delinquency Prevention (OJJDP) National Youth Gang Suppression and Intervention Program was that efforts to reach uniformity in defining gangs continue (Spergel and Chance, 1991). Rather than follow Miller's suggestion to develop a new terminology, Spergel and Chance offered prototype definitions for gangs, posses, crews, and delinquent groups. The major argument against more uniform definitions was voiced by Ruth Horowitz (1990) who emphasized that knowledge of gangs is still too limited to place definitional restrictions on their study. Ball and Curry (1995) have suggested problems in the logic of definition, especially as applied to gangs, may undermine the generation of useful and uniform definitions of gangs and gang problems. A by-product of increased gang legislation emerges in the Institute for Law and Justice (ILJ) report's (1993, p. 3) observation that " every state that has enacted a gang statute has undertaken to define 'gang.' " Uniformity within states may generate new concerns about differences across states.

Linking Causes and Responses

Miller argued that an effective response to America's gang crime problems will require both reliable information and a link between explanation and programs. In their analysis of agency representative responses to a question about the causes of gang crime problems in the agency's community setting, Spergel and Curry (pp. 378) divided perceived causes into four major categories: (1) social system problems, (2) institutional failure, (3) individual or peer-level problems, and (4) response effects. Social system problems include social forces at the social system level such as "poverty, unemployment, criminal opportunities, increased sales and profitability of drugs, patterns of migration and changes in population composition, and other conditions of urban life." As examples of institutional failure, the family and school are most often mentioned. Individual and peer-level problems include "substance abuse, psychological explanations, peer influence, and fear." The final category represents the degree to which elements of reaction programs themselves contribute to or exacerbate gang crime problems. Included there are failures of elements of the criminal justice system, liberalism, failure or inadequacy of social services, media involvement, discrimination, limited community resources, and, ironically, "denial." In Table 7-3 we compare the perceived causes of gang problems with the strategies selected to address them. This table shows that there is no discernible relationship between perceived cause and strategy. The causes of gang crime problems require assessment through sound research, but the link between cause and response is fundamental to program logic.

Table 7-3
Primary Agency Gang Response Strategy by
Primary Perceived Cause of Gang Problems
(Spergel & Curry, 1993, p.380)

	Primary Gang Response Strategy for Agency				
Perceived Primary Cause	Community Organization	Social Intervention	Opportunities Provision	Suppression	Organizational Change/ Development
Social System Cause	10 (9.5%)	26 (24.8%)	7 (6.7%)	48 (45.7%)	14 (13.3%)
Institutional Failure	6 (8.3%)	24 (33.3%)	3 (4.2%)	31 (43.1%)	8 (11.1%)
Individual-Level Cause	3 (9.7%)	11 (35.5%)	0 (0.0%)	14 (45.2%)	3 (9.7%)
Response Effect	3 (9.1%)	16 (48.5%)	1 (3.0%)	11 (33.3%)	2 (6.1%)

Evaluation

Malcolm Klein labels the lack of systematic evaluations of responses to gang crime problems "an inexcusable waste." In answering the question, "Why has the United States failed to solve its youth gang problem?" Walter Miller (1990, p. 272–73) asserts, "The virtual abandonment of sound evaluation of gang control efforts is a major reason for our failure to reduce the gang problems." He argues that "as gang problems have increased, the conduct of program evaluation has decreased." In *Youth Today* (1995), a publication for youth program practitioners, a lead editorial charges that evaluation has failed the needs of practitioners. The editor of *Youth Today* asks, "Dare it be said that the role of evaluation in shaping the nation's youth programs has hit an all time low?"

A particular case in point is the evaluation of the Department of Health and Human Services' Youth Gang Drug Prevention Program. The national evaluation results (Cohen et al., 1995) have received extremely limited circulation and evaluations of consortium project success included no measures at the community level. Instead, surveys of youth with pre-post retrospective questionnaire items and nonsystematic sampling showed "the youth gang drug prevention consortium projects appear to have had little or no influence on participant gang involvement or avoidance" (p. 275).

When the Department of Health and Human Services (DHHS) evaluation process is contrasted with the first recorded evaluation of a gang response project (Thrasher, 1936), it appears sadly lacking. From 1927 to 1931, an evaluation of a gang delinquency prevention project by a large boys' club located in New York City was conducted with $37,500 funding from the Bureau of Social Hygiene. The final report including descriptive, ecological, statistical, and case-study methods was completed in 1935 and found that the club's projects were not an important factor in delinquency prevention and did not reach the "boys that it was designed to serve." In the 1930s example, the practitioners in charge of the agency evaluated were thoroughly briefed on the results and enabled to make programmatic adjustments. There is evidence that NIJ and OJJDP have learned from the failed HHS evaluation approach and that ongoing evaluations of the GREAT (Gang Resistance Educational Assistance Training) program and the OJJDP Comprehensive Response will be subjected to more stringent evaluation in the process of their development.

The Role of Gang Members in Responding to Gang Crime Problems

In offering his "practical agenda" for gang reform, Hagedorn (1988, p. 167) listed as his first principle, "Gang members must participate in any meaningful programs. By 'participate' we mean gang programs need to train and hire former local gang members as staff, utilize older gang members as consultants in developing new programs, and make sure input from the gang 'clients' takes place and is genuine." From their study of communities and crime, Robert

Bursik and Harold Grasmick (1993, p. 177) have suggested "the recruitment of gang members as core members of locally based crime prevention programs." They base this recommendation on gang members' knowledge of crime in the community, gang identification with communities as turf, and a number of historical examples where gang involvement in positive actions have led to short-term reductions in criminal violence.

In the Chicago community of Little Village, Irving Spergel (1994; Spergel and Grossman, 1994) has been working with a network of police, outreach youth workers, probation officers, court service workers, and former gang members to reduce violence between two warring coalitions of Latino street gangs. Preliminary evaluation results of this project indicate a reduction in gang-related homicides, increased community organization and mobilization, and the channeling of gang-involved youths into educational programs and jobs. In Ft. Worth, Texas, as a "last ditch" effort, the city government is supporting the "Comin' Up" program (City of Ft. Worth, 1995). Comin' Up plans to involve 700 gang members in a network of services and activities. Perhaps the most controversial aspect of the Comin' Up program is the hiring of 14 active gang members to serve as outreach workers. In the Chicago community of Englewood, Clemens Bartollas is studying a project in which gang member volunteers serve as disciplinary monitors within community schools (Papajohn and Thomas, 1995; Thomas and Papajohn, 1995). School administrators and community leaders are in full cooperation with the project that treats the gang "as a community group with some redeeming qualities." Gang monitors even have been accorded the authority to levy monetary fines and mete out physical punishment to students who neglect their studies or cause school discipline problems.

In a highly visible book, Arnold Goldstein and Barry Glick (1994) also have challenged Klein's long-standing conclusions on group programming. Goldstein and Glick argue that what Klein and others were measuring in their evaluations of detached street worker programs was a failure of program implementation rather than the ineffectiveness of group programming. Their approach, called "aggression replacement training" (ART), is a group approach that they contend is capable of transforming gangs into prosocial groups. The authors (pp. 92-96) offer process and impact evaluation results to support their conclusions. However, a major concern in interpreting these findings is limited information about the definitions of gang involvement for the delinquent youth tested and the need for structuring controls for variations of gang involvement into the evaluation design. The jury is still out on this approach.

Variations in Gang Crime Problems

Gang responses must take into account variations in the structure and dynamics of gang crime problems that have been observed to exist across municipalities, communities, gender, and ethnicity. Spergel and Curry (1993, pp. 362–63) identified the 45 cities included in the 1988 OJJDP/University of Chicago national survey as either chronic or emerging gang problem cities. This distinction is comparable to the one noted by Moore (1988) and Hagedorn (1988) between "new" and "old" gang cities. Chronic cities were cities where a gang problem was reported to have existed prior to 1980. Emerging cities were those where gang crime problems had only been reported more recently. While chronic gang problem cities tended to be larger cities, such as Los Angeles, Chicago, Philadelphia, and New York City, there were also some smaller cities, especially in California. In chronic gang problem cities, gangs appeared to be better organized and more involved in serious crime, including drug trafficking. There were also differences across chronic and emerging cities in how various antigang response strategies were applied and in how effective responses were perceived to be, particularly in the relationship between community network structures and policy response to gang crime problems. In their analysis of gang homicide and delinquency problems at the community level in Chicago, Curry and Spergel (1988) found significant differences between predominantly African American and predominantly Latino neighborhoods. In their study of gang involvement processes at the individual level, Curry and Spergel (1992) found different models of gang involvement and delinquency for African American youths in comparison to a comparable population of Latino youths residing in close proximity. Hagedorn (1994b) in a study of gang organization in drug selling in three different Milwaukee communities found that organization and behavior varied with neighborhood characteristics. Differences between male and female patterns of gang involvement have been repeatedly observed and documented (Harris, 1988;

Campbell 1991; Moore, 1991; Covey et al., 1992; Joe and Chesney-Lind, 1993; Bjerregaard and Smith, 1993). Additional factors that may condition the peaking of gang involvement include age and geography, as well as variations that emerge within the same community. Not to maintain sensitivity to these community and social differences in gang involvement is to undermine the potential for effectively responding to gang crime problems.

Directions for the Future

In 1971, Malcolm Klein (p. 236) wrote, "Finally, there is the question whether it is even necessary to do gang work. Delinquency in the United States tends to peak at age 16. Gang affiliation similarly peaks at around age 16 or 17. Maturational, cultural, and social forces all combine to bring about a decline in delinquent and gang activity after that time. Shouldn't we be satisfied with this, and put our efforts into areas in which such natural declines do not take place?" We no longer have this option. When comparisons are made between national assessments of the magnitude of the gang crime problem as measured by law enforcement statistics, levels of gang crime problems in terms of numbers of cities with gang problems, gangs, gang members, and gang-related crimes are at all-time highs (Curry, Ball, and Decker, 1995). Gang crime has reached beyond adolescence into young adulthood (Hagedorn, 1988, 1994a) for both males and females and even into the childhoods of new generations (Vigil, 1988; Moore, 1991). The question, then, given what we know about gang response and the gaps in our knowledge is, what should we do now? We offer three recommendations with the comfort of knowing that none of them are completely new.

Continually Evaluate and Improve Evaluation Itself

Despite years of calling for evaluations of gang response programs, the practice of systematic program evaluation is comparatively recent. We must learn how to conduct effective evaluations by repeatedly reflecting on the evaluation process itself. The HHS national-level gang program and the Center for Substance Abuse Prevention (CSAP) required applicants for funding to formulate evaluation plans. From these efforts, we have learned a great deal about how evaluations should be done. The GREAT program and OJJDP's Comprehensive Response have organized independent, appropriately funded independent evaluations. In the 1995-96 NIJ Research Plan (p. 24), the advice on evaluation proposals was specific, "In most instances, the evaluation should be conducted by persons not connected with the implementation of the procedure, training, service, or technique, or the administration of the project." We must also remember that evaluation is not just a tonic to be prescribed for community organization, social intervention, and opportunities provision strategies. It is time for that most frequently applied strategy approach, suppression, to be subjected to systematic evaluation. What we know about the effectiveness of past responses to gang crime problems has been learned by effective evaluation.

Link Response to Theory

In telling us why the United States has failed to solve its youth gang problem, Miller (1990, p. 271) decries the degree to which our response efforts have proceeded without using theory as a tool. One problem is that those who have the ultimate responsibility for developing and implementing programs are policy makers and practitioners who do not have extensive training in theory, while researchers, who have extensive training in theory, do not often have a significant role in the practical aspects of responding to gang problems. Rather, researchers, particularly those who evaluate programs, should take on the responsibility of linking practice to theory. Two excellent examples are readily available. The GREAT program was developed and implemented by practitioners, but the evaluation team of the GREAT program, Winfree, Esbensen, and Osgood, (1995) have carefully and systematically linked the components of the GREAT program to Gottfredson and Hirschi's self-control theory and Akers' social learning theory. Similarly, Spergel and Grossman (1994) began preliminary evaluation of the Little Village Gang Violence Reduction Project by linking program components to several theories, specifically anomie, socialization, differential association, and social control, including community and personal disorganization, in explaining gang-related violence among hardcore older gang youths.

Integrate Response Efforts Institutionally and Historically

We are not advocating that a single federal agency should be responsible for dealing with the national gang problem. Nor do we agree that greater interagency coordination is currently required. However, the kind of communication and cooperation that has been developing at the federal and local levels in the past few years is necessary. Cooperative projects and conferences at the federal level are what we mean by integrating response efforts institutionally. Responding effectively to gang crime problems must be an effort that is marked by an awareness of what has gone before, what is going on elsewhere, and an openness to what can be dreamed.

Summary

The response to gangs and gang-related crime has hardly been well-coordinated, and many interventions have only served to make the problem worse. Responses can be placed into one of five categories: (1) community organization, (2) social intervention, (3) opportunities provision, (4) suppression, and (5) organizational development and change. Evaluation research has found few successes, but opportunities provision appears the most promising category.

Chapter Eight

Gang Theory and Policy

In the early 1980s, researchers spoke of the "end of the youth gang" (Bookin-Weiner and Horowitz, 1983) and Walter Miller's (1982) national surveys were published with a defensive tone that said, "Yes, there are gangs." As we have shown throughout this text, gangs have again become a major concern of researchers and policy makers. In the previous chapter, we reviewed the logic and history of responding to gang problems. In this final chapter, we briefly look at theoretical causes of gang problems and at major contemporary national policy responses to gang problems.

Theories and Gangs

Social Disorganization Theory

As we noted in Chapter 5, a theory that has had recent particular appeal to gang researchers has been William J. Wilson's (1985) concept of an emerging urban underclass population. Wilson's theory has suggested that contemporary inner-city minority residents are segregated and isolated from the economic mainstream in ways that previous poor and minority populations have not been. In the past, all members of minority populations lived in sections of the city segregated by race and ethnicity. While young people growing up in these sections of cities did not have contact with persons of other races, they did have contact with persons of their same race of different social classes. In particular, all young people regardless of race or ethnicity had contact with working adults. In today's urban underclass, Wilson has argued, young people have an increasing likelihood to have no significant contact with working adults in their lives.

Wilson's theory of the urban underclass has been linked to the emergence of gangs by several researchers. In his study of Milwaukee gangs, John Hagedorn (1988) linked the emergence of these gangs to the decline of the city's industrial base. In their study of St. Louis gangs, Scott Decker and Barrik Van Winkle (1996) found that the character of contemporary gang emergence in that city was shaped by patterns of de-industrialization and urban flight by middle- and working-class families. Joan Moore (1989; 1991) emphasized that patterns of gang emergence for Mexican American communities differed from those in African American communities. Still, she has argued that Wilson's urban underclass theory can also be useful in explaining gang problems in Latino communities. In identifying the reason for the proliferation of gang crime problems in recent decades, Malcolm Klein (1995) had suggested that "the spread and deepening of the urban underclass" is one of two major explanatory factors.

Social disorganization theory has a considerably longer history than Wilson's theory of the urban underclass. It was originally applied to gangs by Thrasher (1927) in his studies of Chicago gang youth. For Thrasher, gangs were "interstitial" in the sense that they filled gaps in the institutional fabric in which youths grew into adulthood. Where families or schools were weak or ineffective in socializing a youngster, the gang filled the gaps. Under this theory, strong communities with strong interpersonal ties between neighbors were not settings in which gang problems could develop. The two most prominent researchers who studied gangs in the decades after Thrasher's research were Clifford Shaw and Henry McKay (1943). Through their work and research, social disorganization theory continued to be recognized as the key theory in explaining gang problems and in developing gang policy and programs.

As Robert Bursik and Harold Grasmick (1993) have pointed out, this simple form of social disorganization theory had one great pitfall. This pitfall was clearly identified and critiqued by Ruth Kornhauser (1978) using Chicago communities and gangs as the object of her research. What Kornhauser observed had already begun to trouble Clifford Shaw who had begun to make modifications in social disorganization theory and had joined others in speaking of "differential social organization." The key finding was that gang problems did not emerge only in communities where there were weak personal ties between residents. Many poor inner-city communities had very stable patterns of residency, strong personal ties among community members, *and* persistent gang problems.

In his work with Grasmick and others, Robert Bursik (1993) salvaged social disorganization theory by making some major but significant modifications. Bursik took an idea from Albert Hunter (1985) that there are three levels of community social control in urban settings. The first of these, the personal level of social control, was the corner stone of classic social disorganization theory. Personal social control is based on the interpersonal ties between individual community residents. As Kornhauser (1978) and others had observed, gang and other crime and delinquency problems can still emerge and persist even in communities where levels of personal social control are high.

The two levels of community social control that had been neglected in the earlier version of social disorganization theory were the parochial and public levels. The parochial level of social control consists of ties between community residents and secondary institutions such as schools and businesses. The public level of social control addresses the control of community residents over public resources. Representing political power to exert influence on government and the economy, the public level of social control encompasses such important resources as access to and control over law enforcement and the justice system. While personal social control in a community can be high, low levels of parochial and public social control can result in just that kind of social isolation that is so central to William Wilson's (1987) theory of the urban underclass.

We feel that, largely thanks to the efforts of Bursik and several other theorists, social disorganization theory is once again a major factor in explaining the emergence and persistence of gang problems. It has been central to the development of several of the major gang policy efforts that we examine here.

Subcultural and Values Approaches to Gang Theory

When Clifford Shaw (1943) began to see shortcomings in his version of social disorganization theory, he turned to subcultural explanations. Subcultural theory focuses on values and beliefs among subgroups that differ from those of the mainstream. Shaw suggested that gangs could serve as social mechanisms for transferring deviant normative orientations from older to younger members. Two major versions of subculture theory were put forward to explain gang behavior in the 1950s. Albert Cohen (1955) suggested that gang members fail to succeed in meeting standards of the middle-class value system that they encounter in school. In reaction to this failure, gang members turn the middle-class value system "upside down." The result is a set of negative values that when collectively shared becomes a subculture. The gang is an organizational form of the subculture. The major alternative perspective was offered by Walter Miller (1958), who has been mentioned often in this volume. Miller suggested that gangs are not a reaction to middle-class values; rather, gang life and values grow out of the lower-class norms or focal concerns that gang members share with their parents and other members of the lower class.

A relatively recent version of a subcultural explanation of gang proliferation has been offered by Malcolm Klein (1995). He has argued that gang culture has become part of the nation's mass culture. Gang styles of clothing, moving, and talking have been diffused across the nation by the media and by the migration and travels of youth. According to Klein, copycat behavior can lead to copycat rivalries and conflicts. Overreaction by police to these gangs imitators in smaller cities and towns may only accelerate the process of cohering groups of copycats into full-fledged gangs.

Thomas Winfree is a professor at New Mexico State University. Winfree, with a series of co-authors (1995), has argued that numerous gang researchers have implicitly used the basic tenets of social learning theory and self-control theory without explicitly mentioning these theories. Subcultural theory, in particular, Winfree has argued, has placed the same kinds of emphasis as social learning theory on attitudes and value orientations. Under this perspective, gang involvement is more likely for youth who hold specific preconceptions about what the results of such behavior will be. Such preconceptions are often a function of the values and attitudes that develop through interaction with peers. Similarly, self-control theory holds that gang involvement would be more likely for youths who are impulsive or hedonistic. Under both theories, changes in attitudes and value orientation presage involvement in gang activity.

National Policy and Gangs

At the conclusion of his 1982 national assessment of the nation's gang problem, Walter Miller (1982, p. 149) advised that any significant reduction in collective youth crime would require a major federal initiative. Miller envisioned federal development, support, and monitoring of local efforts. In the late 1980s and the 1990s these kinds of federal initiatives began to be implemented.

The DHHS's Youth Gang Drug Prevention Program

The Omnibus Anti-Drug Abuse Act of 1988 (P.L. 100-690) established the Youth Gang Drug Prevention Program in the Administration on Children, Youth, and Families (ACYF), within the U.S. Department of Health and Human Services (HHS). When applications for the first round of funding were solicited in 1989, priority areas were identified as consortium projects, "single purpose" demonstration projects, and "innovative" support programs for at-risk youths and their families. Of the total of $14.8 million in funding, $9.8 million was awarded to 16 consortium projects (Family and Youth Services Bureau, 1992). A community-based consortium was defined as "a formal partnership among at least three city, county, town, neighborhood, or other local level organizations and/or individuals that have the capacity to generate sustained, collaborative community-wide commitment and support for strategies which address the issues of youth gangs. The organizations could involve voluntary agencies, law enforcement, local government, recreational agencies, youth organizations, businesses, churches, foundations, medical facilities and colleges." Ultimately all 16 of the consortium projects were funded for three years. In design, these programs constituted a federally initiated, coordinated, and monitored commitment to community organization strategic responses to gang crime problems. This commitment was on a scale that was historically without precedent. Nine more consortium projects were funded in 1992 with a total of $5.9 million, each for a period of five years for up to $750,000 per year.

While the consortium projects received the bulk of Youth Gang Drug Prevention Program funding, a number of projects employing social intervention strategies were encompassed by the ACYF program. Over the five years of the program, projects provided peer counseling, family education, youth empowerment, mentoring, crisis intervention, community restitution, and recreation. Priority funding areas for the delivery of services also targeted intergenerational gang families, adolescent females, and new immigrant and refugee youth gangs. (The programs for preventing and reducing gang involvement by adolescent females are discussed in more detail below.) A range of prevention programs were funded in 1992 under the title of "Gangproofing Young Children." In 1992, five projects were funded under the priority area of employment for youth at risk of gang participation. Including projects that cooperated with local private industry councils and trade associations, and programs that helped youths develop entrepreneurial endeavors, this effort incorporated opportunities provision strategies into the coalition of local projects that constituted the national-level of the Youth Gang Drug Prevention Program.

Explicit goals of the Youth Gang Drug Prevention Program mandated by Congress in its creation included facilitating federal, state, and local cooperation and coordination of agencies responding to gang and drug crime problems. Each year between 1991 and 1994, the program sponsored an annual conference designed to build skills, communication, and understanding among representatives of funded projects and other agencies with shared goals. The fourth conference in 1994 encouraged local projects to bring the youths being served by the program to participate in conference activities. In addition to its annual conferences, the program held special focus forums on research, outreach, and new immigrant gangs. A program providing on-site and telephone technical assistance to local agencies nationwide was put in place, and a program newsletter was produced four times each year. Funding solicitations required applicant programs to incorporate a local evaluation plan, and an independent national-level evaluation was funded for the 52 projects initially funded in 1989. The national evaluation (Cohen et al., 1995) concluded that while local programs were generally effective in reducing delinquency and drug use among youth participants, the programs were not successful at preventing or reducing gang involvement. In 1995, the gang component of the program came to an end.

Responding to Female Gang Involvement. One of the components of the Youth Gang Drug Prevention Program included a national-level program that had as primary goals the prevention and intervention of female gang involvement. To our knowledge, it was the only national-level effort that has been devoted specifically to the female gang problem. It owed its existence to the efforts of two women, Joan Moore and Maria Theresa Candamil.

Almost immediately after the decision by Congress to develop the program, staff members at the Family Youth Services Bureau (FYSB) convened a small invited conference of selected researchers and practitioners. The goal of this gathering was to seek input on how the new programs should be structured. In terms of what the program would mean for female gang members, Joan Moore played the most influential role. She recounted her evidence (also included in her 1991 book and reviewed in Chapter 5) that females suffer greater long-term hardships as a result of their adolescent gang involvement than males. She insisted that there be a place in any overall program strategy for specialized programs dedicated to the needs of females. As the program moved into the implementation phase, one administrator at FYSB, Maria Theresa Candamil, played the major role in insuring that programs for females were a part of the FYSB effort. Candamil was central to the design of solicitation for proposals, the awards to sites, and monitoring the component projects of the FYSB Female Gang Prevention and Intervention Program.

Over the six years of its operation, the Female Gang Prevention and Intervention Program awarded funds to 11 projects in 9 cities. The ages of females to be served by the local projects ranged from 8 to 19. The proposed average age of females was 13. Three of the projects targeted African American girls, two targeted Latina females, and one targeted Native American females. The other programs were designed to serve ethnically mixed populations of females. The graphs in Figure 8-1 show ethnic breakdowns for three of the service populations of FYSB program females.

The projects included under the umbrella of the FYSB Female Gang Prevention and Intervention Program varied greatly in organi-

Figure 8-1
*Ethnicity and Race of Females At Risk of Gang Involvement
(Based on data from Programs for Female Gang Prevention)*

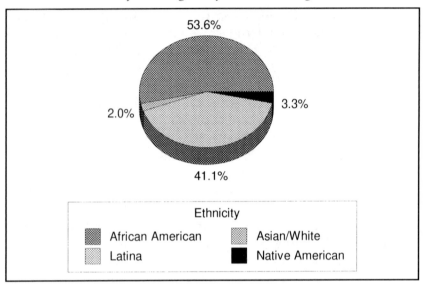

zation and strategy. Case studies and evaluations of three of the projects were conducted by Katherine Williams and Marcia Cohen (1994). Of the three projects, Boston's FORCE program was located in the city's public housing projects. Few of the females served identified themselves as gang members and comparatively few had juvenile records. The program focused on building self-esteem and providing females living in public housing access to structured social activities and recreation. Another program in Seattle served a very small population of females, almost all of whom had been referred to the project by the juvenile court. Slightly more than 40 percent of the females in the Seattle program were former gang members. (Active gang members were not allowed to participate in the program.) The Seattle program placed a heavy emphasis on individual and group counseling and help with completing school and finding employment. Of the females participating in a third project in Pueblo, Colorado, half were current or former gang members. Their levels of contact with the juvenile court fell between that of the females from the other two projects. The Pueblo project offered a wider, more balanced range of services than the other two projects.

Mentoring or one-on-one ties with community adults was central. There was some emphasis on building self-esteem, but there were also major program components on awareness of Mexican American culture and conflict resolution. All three programs have been held up as models by their respective communities, and all have received national attention.

The NIJ Gang Research Initiative

At the 1991 Annual Meetings of the American Society of Criminology, the NIJ (1991) announced its research effort to produce knowledge required for the formulation of national-level responses to gang-related crime. Since its initiation, the NIJ Gang Research Initiative has supported a number of national-level studies of criminal justice system responses to gang-related crime. The results of most of these have been described in this text. The initiative supported Cheryl Maxson and Malcolm Klein's (1994) national-level survey on gang migration and gang structure and their Los Angeles studies of gangs and drug crime. The two national-level surveys of law enforcement information on gang crime problems by Curry and his colleagues, reviewed above, were both funded under the NIJ initiative (Curry et al., 1994, 1995). Other researchers whose work has been funded by the NIJ gang initiative include Ronald Huff, Jeffrey Fagan, Ko-Lin Chin, Susan Pennell, Joan McCord, Jerzy Sarnecki, Terry Miethe, Scott Decker, and James Diego Vigil. As a component of its gang research initiative, NIJ has maintained a special advisory committee on gang issues composed of researchers and practitioners. Each year since 1992, NIJ has sponsored an annual working group meeting that has brought together grantees, advisory committee members, and representatives of other federal agencies responding to gang crime problems. There is no question that the volume of research on gangs has been enhanced by the initiative.

The OJJDP's Comprehensive Response to America's Gang Problem

The funding of the first national assessments of the U.S. gang problem and the 1988 establishment of the National Youth Gang Suppression and Intervention Program by the Office of Juvenile Justice and Delinquency Prevention (OJJDP) have been discussed previously. The suppression and intervention program's goals were "(a) to identify and assess promising approaches and strategies for dealing with the youth gang problem, (b) to develop prototypes or models from the information thereby gained, and (c) to produce technical assistance manuals for those who would implement the models" (Spergel and Curry, 1993, p. 360). The project conducted the national survey of agencies discussed above, conducted a comprehensive review of the literature (Spergel, 1995), conducted symposia of former gang influentials and law enforcement representatives (Spergel et al., 1988; Spergel and Bobrowski, 1990), and conducted site visits to selected programs (Spergel and Chance, 1990). Final products of the project included 12 prototypes or models for gang program development and 12 technical assistance manuals corresponding to each prototype. Initially the products of the program were disseminated on a large scale by the National Youth Gang Information Center, a service that was ultimately transferred to OJJDP's Juvenile Justice Clearinghouse. The major outcome of the project was OJJDP's resolution that community-wide responses were required for dealing with local-level gang problems (Bryant, 1989).

The Spergel Model. By the summer of 1995, the OJJDP formally defined the prototypes and technical assistance manuals produced by Spergel and his collaborators as the Comprehensive Community-Wide Approach to Gangs. More generally the program is identified by policy makers and program practitioners as simply the "Spergel model." In practice, the Spergel model is much more than a complicated program precisely defined by the technical assistance manuals. The Spergel model is an extremely flexible format for responding to gang problems at the community level. Each of the 10 component models represents a potential agency partner. Separate required components focus on community mobilization and employment programs. Any of the component agencies can be the lead or mobilizing agency. Key agencies that must be involved are the police, grassroots organizations, and some form of job program. Otherwise, not all potential components need be involved in every community. The Spergel model was designed to be tailored to the special needs of each individual community. The program's flexibility encourages local program planners to assess the special features of local gang problems and take advantage of local agency strengths. The guidelines for community mobilization are intended to facilitate interagency cooperation and minimize interagency conflict. Under funding from OJJDP, five demonstration sites are in the second year of implementing and testing the Spergel model in a variety of urban settings with coordinated technical assistance and a systematic evaluation led by Spergel himself.

In addition to the five demonstration programs implementing the Spergel model, OJJDP's Comprehensive Response (OJJDP, 1994) established the National Youth Gang Center in Tallahassee, Florida. The Center's 1995 national survey and its results were discussed in Chapter 1. The Center's primary task is to advance the collection and analysis of meaningful gang statistics. In addition to the national surveys, this goal is being pursued by a national-level focus group charged with working toward more uniform definitions and uniform recording of gang-related crime information. Participants in the focus group include representatives of the Federal Bureau of Investigation, the National Drug Intelligence Center, and the National Center for Juvenile Justice. The National Youth Gang Center is also charged with analyzing gang legislation, identifying promising gang program strategies, annually reviewing advances in gang research, and assisting OJJDP in coordinating the activities of the five Spergel model demonstration projects.

The Comprehensive Strategy. At the same time that OJJDP was supporting the development of the Spergel model, separate initiatives were underway to identify the causes and correlates of delinquency and develop systematic program responses to reduce serious, chronic, and violent offending by juveniles. A social development model that incorporated the key influences of family, school, and community and emphasized protective and risk factors emerged (Hawkins, 1996). If serious, chronic, and violent offending was to be reduced, OJJDP (Howell et al., 1995) concluded that the juvenile justice system would have to become part of a comprehensive continuum of services and sanctions. Protective factors would have to be enhanced (not just in the family, but in the womb), and risk factors would have to be diminished or at least mediated. The Comprehensive Strategy, as it is generally known, became official OJJDP policy. Planning grants and funding for demonstration programs were provided to selected sites.

Safe Futures. As the first few years of the 1990s brought record increases in levels of juvenile violence, OJJDP became convinced that the problems of serious, violent, and chronic offending and gang-related crime were related. It was decided that a major effort needed to be undertaken to test both the utility of the Spergel model and the Comprehensive Strategy in specifically targeted geographic settings. The policy result was the Safe Futures program. With funding from OJJDP, Safe Futures Programs have been established in four urban sites (Boston; Seattle; Contra Costa County, California; and St. Louis), one rural site (Imperial Valley, California), and one Indian Reservation (Fort Belknap, Montana). Funding for Safe Futures programs is larger and extended over a longer period of time than funding for previous comparable efforts. Each program is required to incorporate a local evaluation and cooperate with a national evaluation.

Gang Resistance Educational Assistance and Training (GREAT)

In 1991, law enforcement officers from the Phoenix Police Department, in cooperation with local educators and the support of the Bureau of Alcohol, Tobacco, and Firearms (ATF) of the U.S. Treasury Department, developed and initiated a pilot project for a school-based program to provide children in the lower grades with the tools required to resist gang involvement (NIJ, 1994; Esbensen, 1995). Within a year, the program, called Gang Resistance Education Assistance Training (GREAT), had been expanded to include all fourth- and seventh-grade students in Phoenix. GREAT involves a partnership between schools and law enforcement where law enforcement officers train students in resistance skills in school classrooms. By 1994, ATF had entered into 18 cooperative agreements with metropolitan jurisdictions nationwide to provide federal support for the program, and jurisdictions in 33 states were implementing the program without federal support. All GREAT officers are selected competitively by ATF and must undergo two-week training courses. With an ATF officer assigned as a GREAT coordinator at each of ATF's 26 field divisions, ATF centrally coordinates GREAT activities and schedules. In 1994, NIJ in cooperation with ATF funded a multiyear evaluation of GREAT. After a competitive peer review process, a multiuniversity team headed by Finn-Aage Esbensen of the

University of Nebraska was awarded the responsibility of conducting the evaluation, that was mandated to be both longitudinal and cross-sectional in design. The results of the cross-sectional portion of the evaluation have been favorable, suggesting that this program may be having the projected results of preventing gang involvement among program participants (Esbensen et al., 1996).

The COPS Anti-Gang Initiative

Community-oriented policing represents an even broader federal effort to respond to crime in a way that integrates law enforcement into a cooperative community problem-solving framework. In 1996, the Community Oriented Policing Services (COPS) office in the Justice Department launched a 15-city Anti-Gang Initiative. Instead of being selected through a competitive application process, the 15 cities were selected on the basis of their consistency in providing gang-related crime statistics to the Justice Department surveys described above. Funding was to be spent on community policing efforts, to improve data collection, to integrate law enforcement agencies into community-wide responses to gangs, and to provide a safer setting in which less suppressive response programs can be given a chance to develop.

The Future of Gangs

What will be the future of gangs? Will the United States continue to be plagued by the spread of gangs and gang crime? As we look into our crystal ball and attempt to answer this question, it is hard to be optimistic. After all, we have had gangs in America for at least the last hundred years. The good news is that over the last century gangs have come and gone. Gangs flourished in the 1890s, 1920s, 1960s, and now in the 1990s. This historical pattern suggests that gangs are cyclical, coming and going over time. It is reasonable to conclude that gangs will continue to be a feature of American life.

Each time gangs reappear, they reflect the nature of American society. The gangs of the 1890s reflected the urbanization, industrialization, and immigration experienced by a nation just more than one hundred years of age. The social disruption produced by these forces allowed youth gangs to grow and flourish in American cities. By the 1920s, immigrants had established themselves sufficiently to take advantage of the criminal opportunities afforded to gangs by

Prohibition. This meant that both youths and adults were involved in gangs, offering expanded criminal opportunities, as well as the chance for the development of more organized criminal activity. A number of factors intervened to disrupt this stage of gang development, including the Great Depression and World War II. By the 1960s, the struggle of racial minorities in cities helped to fuel a growing gang problem. For the first time, gang activity included substantial numbers of racial and European ethnic minorities. These gangs reflected the segregated nature of cities and opportunities.

Now we face a different set of circumstances. The growth of an urban underclass and rapidly changing economy have created a deeply different state of affairs. There is strong evidence that gangs are spreading well beyond poor, inner-city areas to suburbs and rural areas. This migration of gang ideas and membership is linked to the ability of the media to disseminate gang images through popular culture, such as movies, music videos, and music. The power of popular culture is quite strong and has produced a set of circumstances that finds Crips and Bloods, and Disciples and Kings in rural America as well as such far away settings like New Zealand.

Some commentators (Hagedorn, 1996) argue that gangs have been changed by the dramatic shifts in the American economy. The decline of industry and of the large number of stable jobs (with benefits) provided by an industrial economy have changed life in America. And they have changed gangs. As more adults find themselves without jobs or job prospects, the number of unemployed adults has grown dramatically. This suggests that a vital element missing from most contemporary gangs—motivated adults—could be present as we enter the next century. Industrial jobs have traditionally held out the prospect that a life course into economic sufficiency was attainable. The absence of those jobs means that a growing number of adults, some of whom have been involved in gangs, will no longer find their way into the economy. As a consequence, these individuals will be less likely to form families, less likely to hold full-time employment, and *more* likely to find their way to criminal involvement and ultimately to gangs.

We have talked about the pushes and pulls that affect an individual in deciding to join a gang. Clearly the attractiveness of gangs grows as alternatives to gang life fade. The pushes that compel people to join gangs become stronger in the face of a weak economy.

Confronting gangs, and the forces that create them, will become more important in the years to come. Students like you will play an important role in responding to these challenges.

References

References

Adler, Freda. 1975. *Sisters in Crime: The Rise of the New Female Criminal.* New York: McGraw-Hill.

Alinsky, Saul D. 1946. *Reveille for Radicals.* Chicago: University of Chicago Press.

Asbury, Herbert. 1928. *The Gangs of New York.* Garden City, NY: Alfred Knopf.

Ball, Richard A., and Curry, G. David. 1995. "The Logic of Definition in Criminology: Purposes and Methods for Defining 'Gangs.'" *Criminology* 33: 225–45.

Bibb, Marylyn. 1967. "Gang-Related Services of Mobilization for Youth." In M.W. Klein (ed.), *Juvenile Gangs in Context: Theory, Research, and Action.* Englewood Cliffs, NJ: Prentice-Hall.

Biernacki, P., and Waldorf, D. 1981. "Snowball Sampling: Problems and Techniques of Chain Referral Sampling." *Sociological Methods and Research* 10:141–63.

Bjerregaard, Beth, and Smith, Carolyn. 1993. "Gender Differences in Gang Participation, Delinquency, and Substance Use." *Journal of Quantitative Criminology* 4: 329–55.

Block, Carolyn R., and Block, Richard. 1993. "Street Gang Crime in Chicago." National Institute of Justice Research in Brief. Washington, DC: U.S. Department of Justice.

Bobrowski, Lawrence J. 1988. "Collecting, Organizing and Reporting Street Gang Crime." Paper Presentation. American Society of Criminology Annual Meetings, Chicago.

Bookin-Weiner, Hedy, and Horowitz, Ruth. 1983. "The End of the Gang: Fad or Fact?" *Criminology* 21: 585–602.

Bowker, Lee H., and Klein, Malcolm W. 1983. "The Etiology of Female Juvenile Delinquency and Gang Membership: A Test of Psychological and Social Structural Explanations." *Adolescence* 18: 739–51.

Brown, Waln K. 1977. "Black Female Gang Members in Philadelphia. *International Journal of Offender Therapy and Comparative Criminology* 21: 221–28.

Bryant, Dan. 1989. *Communitywide Responses Crucial for Dealing with Youth Gangs.* Washington, DC: Juvenile Justice Bulletin, Office of Juvenile Justice and Delinquency Prevention, U.S. Department of Justice.

Bursik, Robert J., and Grasmick, Harold G. 1993. *Neighborhoods and Crime: The Dimensions of Effective Community Control.* New York: Lexington Books.

Campbell, Anne. 1981. *Girl Delinquents.* Oxford: Basil Blackwood.

———. 1984, 1991. *The Girls in the Gang,* 2nd ed. Cambridge, MA: Basil Blackwood.

———. 1990. "Female Participation in Gangs." In C. Ronald Huff (ed.), *Gangs in America.* Newbury Park, CA: Sage Publications, 163-182.

Candamil, Maria T. 1992. "Female Gangs: The Forgotten Ones." Washington, DC: Administration for Children, Youth, and Families, U.S. Department of Health and Human Services.

Caplan, Nathan S., Deshaies, Dennis J., Suttles, Gerald D., and Mattick, Hans. 1967. "The Nature, Variety, and Patterning of Street Club Work in an Urban Setting." In Klein, Malcolm (ed.), *Youth Gangs in Context.* Englewood Cliffs, NJ: Prentice Hall.

Chesney-Lind, Meda, 1993. "Girls, Gangs, and Violence: Reinventing the Liberated Female Crook." *Humanity and Society* 17: 321–44.

Chesney-Lind, Meda and Shelden, Randall G. 1992. *Girls: Delinquency and Juvenile Justice.* Pacific Grove, CA: Brooks/Cole.

Chesney-Lind, Meda, Sheldon, Randall G., and Joe, Karen A. 1996. "Girls, Delinquency, and Gang Membership." In C. Ronald Huff (ed.), *Gangs in America.* 2nd Ed. Thousand Oaks, CA: Sage Publications, 185-204.

Chin, Ko-Lin. 1990. *Chinese Subculture and Criminality: Non-traditional Crime Groups in America.* Westport, CT: Greenwood.

City of Fort Worth. 1995. *The Comin' Up Program.* Fort Worth, TX.

Cloward, Richard A., and Ohlin, Lloyd E. 1960. *Delinquency and Opportunity: A Theory of Delinquent Gangs.* New York: Free Press.

Cohen, Albert K. 1955. *Delinquent Boys: The Culture of the Gang.* Glencoe, IL: Free Press.

Cohen, Marcia I., Williams, Katherine, Bekelman, Alan M., and Crosse, Scott. 1995. "Evaluation of the National Youth Gang Drug Prevention Program." In M.W. Klein, C.L. Maxson, and J. Miller (eds.), *The Modern Gang Reader.* Los Angeles: Roxbury Publications, 266–75.

Cook, Thomas D., and Campbell, Donald T. 1979. *Quasi-Experimentation: Design and Analysis Issues for Field Settings*. Boston: Houghton Mifflin.

Cosmos Corporation. 1993. *Forum on the Prevention of Adolescent Female Gang Involvement*. Washington, DC: ACE-Federal Reporters, Inc.

Covey, Herbert C., Menard, Scott, and Franzere, Robert J. 1992. *Juvenile Gangs*. Springfield, IL: Charles C. Thomas.

Cromwell, P., Olson, J., and Avery, D. 1991. *Breaking and Entering*. Beverly Hills, CA: Sage Publications.

Curry, G. David. 1994. *Gang Research in Two Cities*. Final Technical Report Grant #90CL1095. Family Youth Services Bureau, U.S. Department of Health and Human Services.

Curry, G. David, and Spergel, Irving A. 1992. "Gang Involvement and Delinquency among Hispanic and African American Adolescent Males." *Journal of Research on Crime and Delinquency* 29 (No. 3, August): 273–91.

———. 1988. "Gang Homicide, Delinquency, and Community." *Criminology* 26: 381–405.

Curry, G. David, and Thomas, Rodney. 1992. "Community Organization and Gang Policy Response." *Journal of Quantitative Criminology* 8, 4 (December): 357–74.

Curry, G. David, Ball, Richard A., and Decker, Scott H. 1996. "Update on Gang Crime and Law Enforcement Recordkeeping: Report of the 1994 NIJ Extended National Assessment Survey of Law Enforcement Anti-Gang Information Resources." Research Report. National Criminal Justice Reference Service. Washington, DC: U.S. Department of Justice.

Curry, G. David, Ball, Richard A., and Fox, Robert J. 1994a. "Gang Crime and Law Enforcement Recordkeeping." National Institute of Justice Research in Brief. Washington, DC: U.S. Department of Justice.

Curry, G. David, Ball, Richard A, and Fox, Robert J. 1994b. "Criminal Justice Reaction to Gang Violence." In M. Costanzo and S. Oskamp (eds.), *Violence and the Law*. Thousand Oaks, CA: Sage Publications, 203–25.

Curry, G. David, Ball, Richard A., Fox, Robert J., and Stone, Darryl. 1992. "National Assessment of Law Enforcement Anti-Gang Information Resources." Final Report, Washington, DC: National Institute of Justice.

Curry, G. David, Ball, Richard A., Goodnow, Michael H., Egley, Arlen, and Burrus, George. 1997. "Analyses of Available Statistics on Juvenile Hate Crimes." Academy of Criminal Justice Sciences Annual Meetings, Louisville, KY.

Daly, Kathleen, and Chesney-Lind, Meda. 1988. "Feminism and Criminology." *Justice Quarterly* 5: 497–538.

Dawley, David. 1973/1992. *A Nation of Lords : the Autobiography of the Vice Lords.* 2nd ed. Prospect Heights, IL.: Waveland Press; 1st ed., Garden City, NY, Anchor Press.

Decker, Scott H. 1996. "Gangs and Violence: The Expressive Character of Collective Involvement." *Justice Quarterly* 11: 231–50.

Decker, Scott H., and Lauritsen, Janet L. 1996. "Breaking the Bonds of Membership: Leaving the Gang." In C. Ronald Huff (ed.) *Gangs in America.* Second edition. Newbury Park, CA: Sage Publications, 103-122.

Decker, Scott H., and Leonard, Kimberly. 1991. "Constructing Gangs: The Social Construction of Youth Activities." *Criminal Justice Policy Review* 4: 271–291.

Decker, Scott H., and Van Winkle, Barrik. 1994. "'Slinging Dope': The Role of Gangs and Gang Members in Drug Sales." *Justice Quarterly* 11: 583–604.

——. 1996. *Life in the Gang: Family, Friends, and Violence.* New York: Cambridge University Press.

Destro, Robert A. 1993. "Gangs and Civil Rights." In S. Cummings and D.J. Monti (eds.), *Gangs: The Origins and Impact of Contemporary Youth Gangs in the United States.* Albany: State University of New York Press, 277-304.

Duneier, Mitchell. 1992. *Slim's Table: Race, Respectability, and Masculinity.* Chicago: University of Chicago Press.

Esbensen, Finn-Aage. 1995. "Overview of the National Evaluation of GREAT." Presentation at Annual Meetings of the Academy of Criminal Justice Sciences, Boston, MA.

Esbensen, Finn-Aage, and Huizinga, David. 1993. "Gangs, Drugs, and Delinquency in a Survey of Urban Youth." *Criminology* 31, 4 (November): 565–87.

Esbensen, Finn-Aage, Huizinga, David, and Weiher, Anne W. 1993. "Gang and Non-Gang Youth: Differences in Explanatory Factors." *Journal of Contemporary Criminal Justice* 9: 94–116.

Fagan, Jeffrey. 1989. "The Social Organization of Drug Use and Drug Dealing among Urban Gangs." *Criminology* 27,4: 633–69.

——. 1990. "Social Processes of Delinquency and Drug Use Among Urban Gangs." In C. Ronald Huff (ed.), *Gangs in America.* Newbury Park, CA: Sage Publications, 183-219.

——. 1992. "Drug Selling and Licit Income in Distressed Neighborhoods: The Economic Lives of Street-Level Drug Use and Dealers." In A. Harrell and G. Peterson (eds.) *Drugs, Crime and Social Isolation.* Washington, DC: Urban Institute Press, 99–146.

Family and Youth Services Bureau. 1992. *Report to the Congress on the Youth Gang Drug Prevention Program.* Washington, DC: Administration on Children, Youth, and Families, U.S. Department of Health and Human Services.

Felkenes, George T., and Becker, Harold K. 1995. "Female Gang Members: A Growing Issue for Policy Makers." *Journal of Gang Research* 2: 1–10.

Fishman, Laura. T. 1995. "The Vice Queens: An Ethnographic Study of Black Female Gang Behavior." In Malcolm W. Klein, Cheryl L. Maxson, and Jody Miller (eds.), *The Modern Gang Reader.* Los Angeles: Roxbury, 83–92.

Foucault, Michel. 1979. *Discipline and Punish: The Birth of the Prison.* New York: Vintage Books.

Gold, Martin, and Mattick, Hans. 1974. *Experiment in the Streets: the Chicago Youth Development Project.* Ann Arbor: Institute for Social Research, University of Michigan.

Goldstein, Arnold P. 1991. *Delinquent Gangs: A Psychological Perspective.* Champaign, IL: Research Press.

Goldstein, Arnold, and Huff, C. Ronald. 1993. *Gang Intervention Handbook.* Champaign-Urbana, IL: Research Press.

Goldstein, Arnold P., and Glick, Barry, with Carthan, Wilma, and Blancero, Douglas A. 1994. *The Prosocial Gang: Implementing Aggression Replacement Training.* Thousand Oaks, CA: Sage Publications.

Hagedorn, John M. 1988. *People and Folks: Gangs, Crime, and the Underclass in a Rustbelt City.* Chicago: Lakeview Press.

——. 1990. "Back in the Field Again: Gang Research in the Nineties." In C. Ronald Huff (ed.), *Gangs in America.* Newbury Park, CA: Sage Publications, 240–59.

——. 1991a. "Back in the Field Again: Gang Research in the Nineties," in C. Ronald Huff (ed.) *Gangs in America.* Newbury Park, CA: Sage Publications, 240–59.

——. 1991b. "Gangs Neighborhoods and Public Policy." *Social Problems* 38 (4): 529–42.

——. 1994a. "Homeboys, Dope Fiends, Legits, and New Jacks." *Criminology* 32: 197–219.

——. 1994b. "Gangs, Drug Posses, and Neighborhoods." Unpublished manuscript. Urban Research Center, University of Wisconsin, Milwaukee.

Hagedorn, John M., and Devitt, Mary L. 1997. "Fighting Female: The Social Construction of Female Gangs." Unpublished manuscript. The Center for Urban Initiatives and Research. University of Wisconsin-Milwaukee.

Hanson, K. 1964. *Rebels in the Street: The Story of New York's Girl Gangs.* Englewood Cliffs, NJ: Prentice-Hall.

Harris, Mary G. 1988. *Cholas: Latino Girls and Gangs.* New York: AMS.

Hawkins, J. David (ed.) 1996. *Delinquency and Crime: Current Theories.* New York: Cambridge University Press.

Helfgot, Joseph H. 1981. *Professional Reforming: Mobilization for Youth and the Failure of Social Science.* Lexington, MA: Lexington.

Horowitz, Ruth. 1983. *Honor and the American Dream.* New Brunswick, NJ: Rutgers University Press.

——. 1990. "Sociological Perspectives on Gangs: Conflicting Definitions and Concepts." In C. Ronald Huff (ed.), *Gangs in America.* Newbury Park, CA: Sage Publications, 37–54.

Howell, James C. 1994. "Recent Gang Research: Program and Policy Implications." *Crime and Delinquency* 40: 495–515.

Howell, James C., Krisberg, Barry, Hawkins, J. David, and Wilson, John J. 1995. *Serious, Violent, and Chronic Juvenile Offenders: A Sourcebook.* Thousand Oaks, CA: Sage Publications.

Huff, Ronald C. 1989. "Youth Gangs and Public Policy." *Crime and Delinquency* 35: 524–37.

——. 1990. *Gangs in America.* Newbury Park, CA: Sage Publications.

Huizinga, David, Loeber, Rolf, and Thornberry, Terrence P. 1994. "Urban Delinquency and Substance Abuse: Initial Findings." Office of Juvenile Delinquency and Delinquency Prevention.

Hunter, Albert J. 1985. "Private, Parochial, and Public School Orders: The Problem of Crime and Incivility in Urban Communities." In Gerald D. Scuttles and Mayer N. Zald *The Challenge of Social Control: Citizenship and Institution Building in Modern Society.* Norwood, NJ: Ablex Publishing Company.

Hutchison, Ray. 1993. "Blazon Nouveau: Gang Graffiti in the Barrios of Los Angeles and Chicago." In Scott Cummings and Daniel J. Monti (eds.) *Gangs: The Origins and Impact of Contemporary Youth Gangs in the United States.* Albany: State University of New York Press.

Hutchison, Ray and Kyle, Charles. "Hispanic Street Gangs in Chicago's Public Schools." In Scott Cummings and Daniel J. Monti (eds.), *Gangs: The Origins and Impact of Contemporary Youth Gangs in the United States.* Albany: State University of New York Press, 113-136.

Institute for Law and Justice. 1993. "Gang Prosecution Legislative Review." Report prepared for National Institute for Justice, U.S. Department of Justice.

Inter University Consortium for Political and Social Research. 1993. *National Archive of Criminal Justice Data.* Ann Arbor, MI: University of Michigan and Bureau of Justice Statistics.

Jackson, Pamela Irving. 1991. "Crime, Youth Gangs and Urban Transition: The Social Dislocations of Postindustrial Economic Development," *Justice Quarterly* 6: 379–97.

Jackson, Pat, with Rudman, Cary. 1993. "Moral Panic and the Response to Gangs in California." In S. Cummings and D.J. Monti (eds.), *Gangs: The Origins and Impact of Contemporary Youth Gangs in the United States.* Albany: State University of New York Press, 257–75.

Jackson, Robert K., and, McBride, Wesley D. 1986. *Understanding Street Gangs.* Placerville, CA: Copperhouse Publishing.

Joe, Karen, and Chesney-Lind, Meda. 1993. "'Just Every Mother's Angel: an Analysis of Gender and Ethnic Variations in Youth Gang Membership." Paper presented at the annual meeting of the American Society of Criminology, Phoenix, AZ.

———. 1995. "Just Every Mother's Angel: An Analysis of Gender and Ethnic Variations in Youth Gang Membership." *Gender and Society* 9: 408–30.

Kahn, A. J. 1967. "From Delinquency Treatment to Community Development." In P.F. Lazarsfeld, W.H. Sewell, and H.L. Wilensky (eds.), *The Uses of Sociology.* New York: Basic Books, 477–505.

Katz, Jack. 1988. *Seductions of Crime: A Chilling Exploration of the Criminal Mind—From Juvenile Delinquency to Cold-Blooded Murder.* New York: Basic Books.

Klein, Malcolm W. 1969. "On Group Context of Delinquency." *Sociology and Social Research* 54: 63–71.

———. 1971. *Street Gangs and Street Workers.* Englewood Cliffs, NJ: Prentice-Hall.

———. 1995. *The American Street Gang.* New York: Oxford University Press.

Klein, Malcolm and Maxson, C. 1994. "Gangs and Cocaine Trafficking." In D. MacKenzie and C. Uchida (eds.), *Drugs and Crime: Evaluating Public Police Initiatives.* Thousand Oaks, CA.: Sage Publications, 42–58.

———. 1989. "Street Gang Violence." In N. Weiner (ed.), *Violent Crimes, Violent Criminals.* Beverly Hills, CA: Sage Publications, 198–234.

Klein, Malcolm W., Maxson, Cheryl L. and Cunningham, Lea C. 1991. "'Crack,' Street Gangs, and Violence." *Criminology* 29: 623–50.

Kobrin, Solomon. 1959. "The Chicago Area Project — A Twenty-five Year Assessment." *The Annals of the American Academy of Political and Social Science* 322: 1–29.

Kornblum, William S. 1974. *The Blue Collar Community.* Chicago: University of Chicago Press.

Kornhauser, Ruth R. 1978. *Social Sources of Delinquency: An Appraisal of Analytic Models.* Chicago: University of Chicago Press.

Kotlowitz, Alex. 1991. *There Are No Children Here: The Story of Two Boys Growing Up in the Other America.* New York: Doubleday.

Kozol, Jonathan. 1991. *Savage Inequalities: Children in America's Schools.* New York: Crown Publishers.

Kyle, Charles. 1984. *Los Preciosos: The Magnitude of and Reasons for the Hispanic Dropout Problem in Chicago: A Case Study of Two Chicago Public High Schools* Unpublished Ph.D. dissertation, Northwestern University.

Lauderback, David, Hansen, Joy, and Waldorf, Dan. 1992. "Sisters Are Doin' It for Themselves: A Black Female Gang in San Francisco." *The Gang Journal* 1: 57–72.

LeBlanc, A. N. 1994. "While Manny's Locked Up." *New York Times Magazine*, August 14, 26–33, 46–53.

Leonard, Eileen B. 1982. *Women, Crime, and Society: A Critique of Theoretical Criminology.* New York: Longman.

Loftin, Colin. 1984. "Assaultive Violence as Contagious Process." *Bulletin of the New York Academy of Medicine* 62: 550–55.

MacCoun, R. and P. Reuter. 1992. "Are the Wages of Sin $30 an Hour?: Economic Aspects of Street-Level Drug Dealing." *Crime and Delinquency* 38:477–91.

Mann, Coramae R. 1984. *Female Crime and Delinquency.* University, AL: University of Alabama Press.

Mattick, Hans W., and Caplan, Nathan S. "Stake Animals, Loud-Talking, and Leadership in Do-Nothing and Do-Something Situations." In M. W. Klein (ed.), *Juvenile Gangs in Context: Theory Research and Action.* Englewood Cliffs, NJ: Prentice-Hall, 106–19.

Maxson, Cheryl L. 1995. "Research in Brief: Street Gangs and Drug Sales in Two Suburban Cities." In Malcolm W. Klein, Cheryl L. Maxson, and Jody Miller (eds.), *The Modern Gang Reader.* Los Angeles: Roxbury, 228–35.

Maxson, Cheryl L., and Klein, Malcolm W. 1990. "Street Gang Violence: Twice as Great, or Half as Great." In C. Ronald Huff (ed.), *Gangs in America.* Newbury Park, CA: Sage Publications, 71–100.

——. 1994. "The Scope of Street Gang Migration in the U.S." Presentation. Gangs Working Group. National Institute of Justice.

Maxson, Cheryl L., Gordon, M.A., and Klein, Malcolm W. 1985. "Differences between Gang and Nongang Homicides." *Criminology* 23: 209–22.

Maxson, Cheryl L., Klein, Malcolm W., and Cunningham, Lea C. 1992. "Street Gangs and Drug Sales." Report to the National Institute of Justice.

Maxson, Cheryl L., Klein, Malcolm, and Gordon, Margaret A. 1990. "Street Gang Violence as a Generalizable Pattern." Unpublished paper. University of Southern California, Social Science Research Institute.

McCord, Joan. 1994. "Delinquent Networks in Philadelphia." Paper presentation. American Society of Criminology Annual Meetings, Miami, Florida.

Merton, Robert K. 1957. *Social Theory and Social Structure*, rev. ed. Glencoe, IL: Free Press.

Mieczkowski, T. 1986. "Geeking Up and Throwing Down: Heroin Street Life in Detroit." *Criminology* 24:645–66.

Miller, Jody. 1996. "Gender and Victimization Risk among Young Women in Gangs." Paper presented at the Annual Meeting of the American Society of Criminology, Chicago, November 21.

Miller, Walter B. 1958. "Lower Class Culture as a Generating Milieu of Gang Delinquency." *Journal of Social Issues* 14: 5–19.

——.1962 "The Impact of a 'Total Community' Delinquency Control Project." *Social Problems* 19: 168–191.

——. 1973. "The Molls." *Society* 11: 32–35.

——. 1975. *Violence by Youth Gangs and Youth Groups as a Crime Problem in Major American Cities*. Washington, DC: U.S. Government Printing Office.

——. 1982. *Crime by Youth Gangs and Groups in the United States*. Washington, DC: National Institute of Juvenile Justice and Delinquency Prevention, U.S. Department of Justice.

——. 1990. "Why the United States Has Failed to Solve Its Youth Gang Problem." In C. Ronald Huff (ed.), *Gangs in America*. Newbury Park, CA: Sage Publications, 263–87.

——. 1997. *The Growth of Youth Gang Problems in the United States 1970-1995*. Draft Report. National Youth Gang Center, Tallahassee, Florida.

Monti, Daniel J. 1993. "Origins and Problems of Gang Research in the United States." In S. Cummings and D.J. Monti (eds.), *Gangs: The Ori-*

gins and Impact of Contemporary Youth Gangs in the United States. Albany: State University of New York Press, 3–25.

Moore, Joan W. 1978. *Homeboys: Gangs, Drugs, and Prison in the Barrios of Los Angeles*. Philadelphia: Temple University Press.

———. 1988. "Introduction." In John M. Hagedorn, *People and Folks: Gangs, Crime, and the Underclass in a Rustbelt City*. Chicago: Lakeview Press.

———. 1989. "Is There an Hispanic Underclass?" *Social Science Quarterly* 70: 265–83.

———. 1990. "Gangs, Drugs and Violence", in M. De La Rosa, E. Lambert, and B. Gropper (eds.), *Drugs and Violence: Causes, Correlates and Consequences*. Washington, DC: NIDA, 160–176.

———. 1991. *Going Down to the Barrio: Homeboys and Homegirls in Change*. Philadelphia: Temple University Press.

———. 1993. "Gangs, Drugs, and Violence." In S. Cummings and D.J. Monti (eds.), *Gangs: The Origins and Impact of Contemporary Youth Gangs in the United States*. Albany: State University of New York Press, 27–46.

Moore, Joan W., and Hagedorn, John M., 1996. "What Happens to Girls in the Gang?" In C. Ronald Huff (ed.), *Gangs in America*, 2nd ed. Thousand Oaks, CA: Sage Publications, 205-218.

National Institute of Justice. 1991. *National Institute of Justice Research on Gangs*. Washington, DC: U.S. Department of the Justice, Office of Justice Programs.

———. 1992. *Action Plan Development for Gangs Initiative*. Washington, DC: U.S. Department of the Justice, Office of Justice Programs.

———. 1993a. *NIJ Program Plan*. Washington, DC: U.S. Department of Justice

———. 1993b. *Gangs Initiative Planning Proceedings*. Washington, DC: National Institute of Justice.

———. 1994a. *Gangs Initiative Planning Proceedings*. Washington, DC: National Institute of Justice.

———. 1994b. *Solicitation for an Evaluation of G.R.E.A.T.: Gang Resistance Education and Training*. Washington, DC: U.S. Department of the Justice, Office of Justice Programs.

———. 1995. *NIJ Research Plan 1995-1996*. Washington, DC: U.S. Department of the Justice, Office of Justice Programs.

Needle, Jerome, and Stapleton, W. Vaughan. 1983. *Report of the National Juvenile Justice Assessment Centers, Police Handling of Youth Gangs*. Washington, DC: Office of Juvenile Justice and Delinquency Prevention, U.S. Department of Justice.

Office of Juvenile Justice and Delinquency Prevention. 1994. *FY 1994 Discretionary Competitive Program Announcements.* Washington, DC: U.S. Department of the Justice, Office of Justice Programs.

Padilla, Felix M. 1992. *The Gang as an America Enterprise.* New Brunswick, N.J: Rutgers University Press.

Papajohn, George, and Thomas, Jerry. 1995. "School Monitors Are Gang Members." *Chicago Tribune* (June 15): 1, 8.

Perkins, Useni Eugene. 1987. *Explosion of Chicago's Black Street Gangs.* Chicago: Third World Press.

Quicker, John C. 1983. *Homegirls: Characterizing Female Gangs.* San Pedro, CA: International University Press.

Reiner, I. 1992. "Gangs, Crime and Violence in Los Angeles." Office of the District Attorney, County of Los Angeles. May 1992.

Rice, Robert. 1963. "A Reporter at Large: The Persian Queens." *The New Yorker* 39: 139 ff.

Roberts, Albert R. 1989. *Juvenile Justice: Policies, Programs, and Services.* Chicago: Dorsey Press.

Sanchez-Jankowski, Martin. 1991. *Islands in the Street: Gangs and American Urban Society.* Berkeley: University of California Press.

Sale, Richard T. 1972. "The Blackstone Rangers: A Reporters Account of Time Spent With the Street Gang on Chicago's South Side. New York: Random House.

Sanders, William. 1994. *Drive-bys and Gang Bangs: Gangs and Grounded Culture.* New York: Aldine de Gruyter.

Schlossman, Steven, and Sedlak, Michael. 1983. "The Chicago Area Project Revisited." *Crime and Delinquency* 29: 398–462.

Shaw, Clifford R., and McKay, Henry D. 1943. *Juvenile Delinquency and Urban Areas.* Chicago: University of Chicago Press.

Sheley, Joseph, Shang, Joseph, and Wright, James. 1993. "Gang Organization, Routine Criminal Activity, and Gang Member's Criminal Behavior." A Report to the National Institute of Justice and the Office of Juvenile Justice and Delinquency Prevention.

Short, James F., Jr. 1974. "Collective Behavior, Crime and Delinquency." In D. Glaser (ed.), *Handbook of Criminology.* New York: Rand McNally, 403–49.

———. 1985. "The Level of Explanation of Problem," in R. Meier (ed), *Theoretical Methods in Criminology.* Beverly Hills, CA: Sage Publications, 51–72.

Short, James F., Jr., and, Strodtbeck, Fred L. 1965. (1974, 2nd ed.) *Group Process and Gang Delinquency.* Chicago: University of Chicago Press.

Siegel, Taggert, and Conquergood, Dwight. 1990. *Heart Broken in Half.* Chicago: Siegel Productions.

Simon, Rita J. 1975. *Women and Crime.* Lexington, MA: Lexington Books.

Skolnick, Jerome. 1990. "The Social Structure of Street Drug Dealing." *American Journal of Police* 9:1–41.

Skolnick, Jerome, Correl, T., Navarro, E., and Robb, R. 1988. "The Social Structure of Street Drug Dealing." BCS Forum. Office of the Attorney General, State of California.

Spergel, Irving A. 1964. *Racketville, Slumtown, Haulburg.* Chicago: University of Chicago Press.

———. 1966. *Street Gang Work: Theory and Practice.* Reading, MA: Addison-Wesley.

———. 1969. *Community Problem Solving: The Delinquency Example.* Chicago: University of Chicago Press.

———. 1972. "Community Action Research as a Political Process." In I.A. Spergel (ed.), *Community Organization: Studies in Constraint.* Beverly Hills, CA: Sage Publications, 231–62.

———. 1985. *Youth Gang Activity and the Chicago Public Schools.* Chicago: University of Chicago, School of Social Service Administration.

———. 1990. "Youth Gangs: Continuity and Change." In M. Tonry and N. Morris, *Crime and Justice: A Review of Research.* Vol. 12. Chicago: University of Chicago Press.

———. 1984. "Violent Gangs in Chicago: In Search of Social Policy." *Social Service Review* 58: 199–226.

———. 1994. Submitted Testimony of I.A. Spergel. Hearing on Gang Crime, Subcommittee on Juvenile Justice, U.S. Senate Committee on the Judiciary (Feb. 9).

———. 1995. *The Youth Gang Problem: A Community Approach.* New York: Oxford University Press.

Spergel, Irving A., and Bobrowski, Lawrence. 1990. *Law Enforcement Definitional Conference Transcript.* Washington, DC: Juvenile Justice Clearinghouse, Office of Juvenile Justice and Delinquency Prevention.

Spergel, Irving A., and Chance, Ronald L. 1991. "National Youth Gang Suppression and Intervention Program." *NIJ Reports* 224: 21–24.

———. 1990. *Community and Institutional Responses to the Youth Gang Problem.* Washington, DC: Juvenile Justice Clearinghouse, Office of Juvenile Justice and Delinquency Prevention.

Spergel, Irving A., and Curry, G. David. 1989. "Socialization to Gangs: School-Community Gang Prevention and Control Study." Research Report. School of Social Service Administration, University of Chicago.

———. 1990. "Strategies and Perceived Agency Effectiveness in Dealing with the Youth Gang Problem." In C.Ronald Huff (ed.), *Gangs in America.* Newbury Park, CA: Sage Publications, 288–309.

———. 1993. "The National Youth Gang Survey: A Research and Development Process." In Arnold Goldstein and C. Ronald Huff (eds.). *Gang Intervention Handbook.* Champaign-Urbana: Research Press, 359-400.

Spergel, Irving A. and Grossman, Susan F. 1994. "Gang Violence and Crime Theory: Gang Violence Regduction Project." Presentation. American Society of Criminology Annual Meetings. Miami, FL.

Spergel, Irving A., Cane, Candace, Chance, Ronald L., Hyatt, Michael, Ross, Ruth, and Rodriguez, Pamela. 1988. *Report of the Law Enforcement Youth Gang Symposium.* Washington, DC: Juvenile Justice Clearinghouse, Office of Juvenile Justice and Delinquency Prevention.

Spergel, Irving A., Chance, Ronald L., Ehrensaft, K., Regulus, Tom, Kane, Candace, and Alexander, A. 1992a.*Prototype/Models for Gang Intervention and Suppression.* Washington, DC: Juvenile Justice Clearinghouse.

Spergel, Irving A., Chance, Ronald L., Ehrensaft, K., Regulus, Tom, Kane, Candace, and Laseter, R. 1992b. *Technical Assistance Manuals.* Washington, DC: Juvenile Justice Clearinghouse.

Sutherland, Edwin H. 1947. *Principles of Criminology.* New York: J.B. Lippincott Company.

Taylor, Carl. 1990. *Dangerous Society.* East Lansing: Michigan State University Press.

———. 1993. *Girls, Gangs, Women and Drugs.* East Lansing, MI: Michigan State University Press.

Thomas, Jerry, and Papajohn, George. 1995. "Monitors Recruited from Streets." *Chicago Tribune* (June 15): 8.

Thornberry, Terrence, Krohn, Marvin D., Lizotte, Alan J., and Chard-Wierschem, Deborah. 1993. "The Role of Juvenile Gangs in Facilitating Delinquent Behavior." *Journal of Research in Crime and Delinquency* 30: 55–87.

Thrasher, Frederic. 1927. *The Gang: A Study of 1,313 Gangs in Chicago.* Chicago: University of Chicago Press.

———. 1936. "The Boys Club and Juvenile Delinquency." *American Journal of Sociology* 41: 66–80.

Toobin, Jeffrey. 1994. "Capone's Revenge," *New Yorker*, May 23: 46-59.

Tromanhauser, Edward F., Corcoran, Tom, and Lollino, Allen. 1981. *The Chicago Safe School Study.* Chicago: City of Chicago, Chicago Board of Education.

Venkatesh, Sudhir Alladi. 1997. "The Social Organization of Street Gang Activity in an Urban Ghetto." *American Journal of Sociology* 101: 82-111.

Vigil, James Diego. 1988. *Barrio Gangs.* Austin: University of Texas Press.

Vigil, James Diego. 1990. "Emic and Etic Perspectives of Gang Culture: The Chicano Case." In C. R. Huff (ed.) *Gangs in America.* Newbury Park, CA: Sage Publications, 55-68.

Weiss, Carolyn. 1993. "Gender Research of Economic Development Planning." Presentation. Regional Research Institute, West Virginia University, Morgantown, WV.

Whyte, William F. 1943. *Street Corner Society.* Chicago: University of Chicago Press.

Williams, Katherine, Cohen, Marcia, and Curry, G. David. 1994. "Evaluation of Female Gang Prevention Programs." Presentation. American Society of Criminology Annual Meetings. Miami, FL.

Wilson, William J. 1987. *The Truly Disadvantaged.* Chicago: University of Chicago Press.

———. 1996. *When Work Disappears: The World of the New Urban Poor.* New York: Alfred A. Knopf.

Winfree, L. Thomas, Jr., Esbensen, Finn-Aage, and Osgood, D. Wayne. 1995. "On Becoming a Youth Gang Member: Low Self-Control or Learned Behavior?" Presentation at Annual Meetings of the Academy of Criminal Justice Sciences, Boston, MA.

Wright, Richard, and Decker, Scott H. 1994. *Burglars on the Job: Streetlife and Residential Burglary.* Boston: Northeastern University Press.

Wright, R., Decker, S., Redfern, A., and Smith, D. 1992. "A Snowball's Chance in Hell: Doing Field Research with Active Offenders." *Journal of Research in Crime and Delinquency* 29:148–61.

Yablonsky, Lewis. 1959. "The Gang as a Near-Group." *Social Problems.* 7: 108–17.

———. 1962. *The Violent Gang.* Baltimore: Penguin. *Youth Today: The Newspaper on Youth Work.*

———. 1995. "Evaluating the Evaluators." Vol. 4, No. 3, May/June, 2.

Youth Today: The Newspaper on Youth Work. 1995. "Evaluating the Evaluators," editorial. Vol. 4, No. 3, May/June 1995.

Subject
and
Author
Indexes

Author Index

R

Reiner, I., 87, 92
Reuter, P., 93
Roberts, A. R., 145
Rossi, 151
Rudman, C., 152

S

Sanchez-Jankowski, M., 43, 54,
    62, 84, 85–86,
    91, 93, 136, 139
Sanders, W., 4, 5, 50, 90, 92, 93
Sarnecki, J., 173
Schlossman, S., 145–146
Sedlak, M., 145–146
Shang, J., 88
Shaw, C., 144–145, 166, 167–168
Shelden, R., 97, 117
Sheley, J., 88
Short, J. F., 34, 41, 44, 50, 84, 91–92
Siegel, T., 4
Skolnick, J., 62, 84, 85, 91, 92, 93
Smith, C., 52, 119, 161
Spergel, I., 3, 4, 20, 33, 47, 49, 50–
    51, 55, 58, 93, 97, 113, 114, 115,
    128, 130, 134–135, 136–137,
    138, 142–143, 147, 148, 149,
    150, 151, 153, 155, 156, 157,
    159, 160, 162, 174
Stapleton, W. V., 19, 47, 147
Strodtbeck, F. L., 34, 41, 50, 92

T

Taylor, C., 42, 54, 86, 91, 93, 117
Thomas, J., 159
Thornberry, T., 51, 55, 73
Thrasher, vi, 30, 31–32, 41, 58, 97,
    100–103, 112, 114, 121, 128,
    130, 131, 134, 135, 136, 138,
    144, 152, 153, 158, 166
Toobin, 26
Tromanhauser, E., 127

V

Van Winkle, 6, 25, 44, 45, 63, 70,
    74, 84, 90, 91, 115, 116, 125,
    129–130, 131, 136, 138, 139,
    164
Venkatesh, S., 46
Vigil, J. D., 40, 43, 58, 63, 92, 124,
    125,
    131, 161, 173

W

Waldorf, D., 115, 117
Weiher, 51, 55
Whyte, W. F., 32, 115
Williams, K., 169
Wilson, W. J., 115, 124, 126, 137,
    165–166, 167
Winfree, L. T., 162, 168
Wright, J., 88

Y

Yablonsky, L., 32, 53

Subject Index